THE BIBLE CRASH COURSE
FOR THE SUNDAY SCHOOL

THE BIBLE CRASH COURSE
FOR THE SUNDAY SCHOOL

ROBYN DOWNEY

WESTBOW
PRESS®
A DIVISION OF THOMAS NELSON
& ZONDERVAN

WestBow Press books may be ordered through booksellers or by contacting:

WestBow Press
A Division of Thomas Nelson & Zondervan
1663 Liberty Drive
Bloomington, IN 47403
www.westbowpress.com
1 (866) 928-1240

Interior graphics: April Borchelt

ISBN: 978-1-5127-7226-5 (sc)
ISBN: 978-1-5127-7228-9 (hc)
ISBN: 978-1-5127-7227-2 (e)

Library of Congress Control Number: 2017900608

Print information available on the last page.

WestBow Press rev. date: 2/6/2017

CONTENTS

"Do you understand what you are reading?" Philip asked.
"How can I," he said, "unless someone explains it to me?"
So he invited Philip to come up and sit with him.
—ACTS 8:30–31

Even a biblical person who was reading the Bible had trouble understanding it. So don't feel alone!

INTRODUCTION

YEARS AGO I WOULD SIT IN CHURCH, LISTENING TO THE
pastor and paying attention to the sermon. The Bible would be
quoted. I would understand the lesson, the meaning of the sermon.
But I didn't understand the Bible. "You will not fear the terror of
night, nor the arrow that flies by day" (Psalm 91:5). *Hmmm*, I would
think. I had so many questions. Where is this in the Bible? Where is
this in the story? Who said it and when?

Every Sunday I vowed to go home and immediately read the Bible
cover to cover. You guessed it. I never did. But I did begin learning
and studying the Bible. And if you're like me, who grew up and never
made it to two Sunday school lessons in a row, this book is for you.
By the end, you will have a better sense of the chronological order of
the Bible, and your Sundays in church will be more valuable because
you'll have a richer understanding of the Bible.

Each chapter of this book will take you through the Bible
chronologically. Discussion questions will be at the end of every
section. Once you've mastered this, you'll be able to read, study, and
discuss the Bible on your own with more confidence. And just like
Christianity, good things will blossom more good things. I hope
you're excited to begin the journey!

BIBLE BASICS

OVER THE CENTURIES, MANY VERSIONS OF THE BIBLE HAVE emerged. I personally like the New International Version (NIV) because I find it the easiest to read. I'll be referencing this version throughout.

The Bible is not necessarily in chronological order, and many authors wrote it over the centuries. You'll also discover some information repeated in various books of the Bible from different vantage points.

But before we begin to examine the Bible more deeply, I'll start with some basic information. The Bible is comprised of books, sixty-six in total. The Old Testament has thirty-nine books; the New Testament has twenty-seven books.

Covering thousands of years of history, the Old Testament tells the story of the Hebrew people and their relationship with God. You'll find history, poetry, and prophecy. The first five books are sometimes called "the books of Moses" because he wrote them. Jesus referred to these books as "the law." The oldest books, they begin with creation.

The next twelve books pass down the history of the Jewish people. The following five consist of beautiful poetry, Psalms and Proverbs among them. Next you'll find seventeen prophetical books, which, generally speaking, warn the Hebrews about their sins and foretell God's consequences for these sins.

Between the Old and New Testaments, you'll find four hundred years of silence. God is quietly working during this time, and I like to call it the "intermission" of the Bible.

The New Testament begins with the birth and life of Jesus. The first four books are called the Gospels, and they tell His story from four different points of view. The next book is Acts, also called Acts of the Apostles. Jesus has died and has risen from the dead, and Acts recounts how the early church is established after Christ's resurrection. Several people wrote the last twenty-two books. Twenty-one of these are letters. Paul wrote thirteen of them. The last book of the Bible, Revelation, is apocalyptic writing, which means to reveal hidden information.

SETTING THE STAGE

BEFORE ABOUT 3000 BC, PEOPLE LIVED IN GROUPS AND traveled together, following animal herds and seasonal plants for food. This nomadic lifestyle, also known as hunting and gathering, didn't support any real technological advancement. An area of the modern-day Middle East changed all that.

In the fertile soil of the land between two rivers, known as Mesopotamia or the Fertile Crescent, settlements began to form. People grew their own food, built houses, traded, and organized governments. Much of the Bible takes place in this relatively small location. If you look at a current map of the area, you'll find the countries of Israel, Syria, Iraq, Jordan, Turkey, and Saudi Arabia. Egypt and areas around the Mediterranean Rim and Rome, Italy, are also part of the Bible.

When people needed to go somewhere, traveling was hard. They walked or rode animals, and the voyages were long and dangerous. Please refer to the appendix maps to assist you as we follow the journeys of the biblical people.

THE OLD TESTAMENT

CREATION AND THE
PATRIARCH

"IN THE BEGINNING GOD CREATED THE HEAVENS AND THE earth" (Genesis 1:1). The Bible begins with the book of Genesis, generally accepted as written by Moses. The accounts of creation, Adam and Eve, Noah, and the Tower of Babel take place during prehistory. The story of the patriarch, Abram, marks the origin of historical events.

God creates everything in the first six days, and on the seventh day, He rests. On the sixth day, God creates man in His own image, "So God created man in his own image, in the image of God he created him; male and female he created them" (Genesis 1:27).

Adam and Eve live in the garden of Eden, believed to be located near the mouth of the Tigris and Euphrates Rivers. Unfortunately sin enters the scene and destroys God's original plan for us. The serpent tempts Eve to eat from the Tree of Knowledge of Good and Evil. Adam and Eve both eat from this tree, which God has strictly forbidden. Their rebellion against God is the original sin that separates us from Him.

As time passes, Adam and Eve have children. Their son Cain

kills his brother Abel, and sin continues through generations of humankind. God decides to cleanse the earth with a great flood, saving only Noah, members of his family, and enough animals to repopulate the world.

Noah's family begins to multiply, and sin again infiltrates. The people decide to build a tower to heaven in self-celebration. The people all spoke the same language so God decides to confuse the language among them. Now that people all speak different languages, they wander and scatter, abandoning the self-indulgent project.

Ten generations after Noah, Abram is born in the land of Ur, an area probably located near the Tigris and Euphrates Rivers. God handpicks Abram as the patriarch of the Hebrew nation, one that will represent God in the world. Once God creates the covenant between Himself and Abram, He changes Abram's name to Abraham. Abraham and his wife Sarah are instructed to leave Ur and travel a great distance to a land called Canaan along the east coast of the Mediterranean Sea. They are very old and have never had children. God is making big promises, and they find it incredible, if not humorous, that they should become parents at their ages.

Sarah decides to hurry along God's plan by giving her servant Hagar to Abraham to sleep with. Hagar becomes pregnant and gives birth to a son, Ishmael. Hagar and Ishmael are sent away because of Sarah's jealousy, but God takes care of them, and Ishmael ultimately becomes the father of the Arab people.

To her surprise, Sarah does become pregnant and gives birth to a boy, Isaac, the child God has intended to carry on the lineage of the new nation. In a great test of Abraham's faith, the Lord tells Abraham to offer Isaac as a sacrifice. Out of pure obedience and trust in God, Abraham prepares to offer his promised son to the Lord. Just before doing so, God interrupts the sacrifice, having determined Abraham's obedience to Him.

Isaac grows up and marries a young woman, Rebekah, who eventually becomes pregnant with twins who fight with each other inside her womb. The Lord tells her that there are two nations in her womb, and she gives birth to Jacob and Esau.

Esau grows up to father a nation, Edom, located to the south of Canaan. The Edomites are all descendants of Esau. Jacob is part of the original covenant with his grandfather Abraham to populate a new nation with his offspring.

When Jacob becomes older, he goes to work for Laban. Jacob soon falls in love with Laban's second-oldest daughter, Rachel. In exchange for her hand in marriage, Jacob agrees to work for Laban for seven years. At the end of the seven years, a great wedding celebration takes place, but unfortunately for Jacob, Laban secretly switches Rachel for his oldest daughter, Leah. Jacob eventually agrees to work seven more years to marry Rachel as well.

Years pass, and even though Rachel seems to be barren, God blesses Leah with many sons. Finally the Lord does give Rachel two sons, Joseph and Benjamin. Altogether, Jacob has twelve sons and one daughter with Leah, Rachel, and their maid servants. The twelve sons ultimately become the twelve tribes of Israel.

Two of Jacob's sons, Judah and Joseph, should be highlighted in this narrative. Judah marries off his son to Tamar. Unfortunately Tamar's husband dies, so she is given to the next son in marriage, as is custom. He dies as well. Out of fear of losing another, Judah refuses to give another one of his sons to Tamar.

Tamar, alone and desperate, poses as the temple prostitute to trick Judah into sleeping with her. Months later, she is discovered to be pregnant, and Judah almost murders her until she reveals her own identity and his identity as the father of her children, twin boys, Perez and Zerah.

Joseph's brothers are jealous of the favor that Jacob shows to him, so they concoct a plan to kill him. The plan goes awry, and they sell him to some Egyptians passing by. Jacob believes his son is dead while Joseph spends many years in Egypt. Joseph, a slave, is imprisoned and then becomes a trusted adviser and second-in-command to the Pharaoh. Blessed with a gift for dream interpretation, Joseph is able to prepare Egypt for seven years of famine.

While his brothers and father are struggling back home in Canaan, Joseph successfully plans for the hardship. Jacob sends his remaining sons to Egypt to ask for help getting through the drought. In a turn of events, the brothers bow to Joseph, not knowing his true identity. In time, Joseph reveals himself to his brothers. And with no animosity, all is forgiven. All brothers and Jacob are invited to live in Egypt.

There are two important points of the Patriarch story:

1. God uses unlikely and often imperfect individuals to accomplish His work in the world.

2. The patriarch and family line is the lineage leading to the birth of Jesus Christ.

DISCUSSION QUESTIONS

1. In Genesis 1:27, God creates man in the image of Himself. In what ways have you observed God's imprint on you? Consider how you interact with family, friends, coworkers, and strangers.

2. After the original sin, Adam and Eve eat the fruit of the forbidden tree and hide from God in shame. "But the Lord God called to the man, 'Where are you?'" (Genesis 3:9). God knows everything. He knew where they were and what had happened. He could have just turned away. But God doesn't turn away. He calls out to them and looks for them. God continues to call to His people throughout the Bible. He wants us back. Is this something you have ever thought about?

3. Jacob favors his wife Rachel over Leah, yet the Lord remembers Leah by blessing her with many sons. Have you ever felt rejected by others yet remembered by the Lord? In what ways?

4. The lineage to Jesus Christ will be through Judah and not Joseph. What are your thoughts on why God might have chosen a less perfect person in line to Christ?

EXODUS AND CONQUEST
OF THE PROMISED LAND

THIS CHAPTER WILL COVER THE REMAINING BOOKS OF
Moses, along with the book of Joshua. Moses wrote Exodus, Leviticus,
Numbers, and Deuteronomy. Joshua himself wrote most of the book
of Joshua.

As the book of Exodus opens, the descendants of Jacob have
become quite numerous and pose a perceived threat to the Pharaoh.
The Pharaoh, who is not named in the Bible, enslaves the Israelites
in order to control their numbers. The exact date of the Exodus is
a debated issue since the Pharaoh is unnamed. Some Bible quotes
place Exodus at 1440 BC while others place it at about 1240 BC, two
hundred years later.

In an extreme attempt to limit the number of Israelites, Pharaoh
orders all newborn Hebrew males be killed. The midwives refuse to
obey this order. Jochebed gives birth to a baby boy and hides him
for three months. Unable to hide him any longer, she places him in
the river near the place where the Pharaoh's daughter bathes. The
baby's sister, Miriam, watches in secret as her brother is discovered.
Pharaoh's daughter realizes he is a Hebrew baby, and she takes him in.

Miriam approaches Pharaoh's daughter and offers a Hebrew woman (her own mother) to nurse the baby for her. She accepts.

The baby is named Moses, which means "to draw out of the water." Moses grows to adulthood in the house of Pharaoh. One day, he witnesses an Egyptian and a Hebrew fighting, and Moses kills the Egyptian. Now Moses is in trouble and flees to Midian, where he spends many years. Moses marries a shepherd's daughter and has a son.

God hears the continued suffering of the Hebrew slaves in Egypt, and He appears to Moses in the form of burning bush that the fire does not consume. God tells Moses to leave, go to Egypt, and lead His chosen people to the Promised Land of Canaan. Moses is nervous to speak to Pharaoh, so God allows both Moses and his brother Aaron to go before Pharaoh with the instructions from God.

Upon hearing the request to allow his slaves to leave Egypt for the Promised Land, Pharaoh's heart is hardened. He refuses, so God responds with ten plagues to curse Egypt. The first nine plagues consist of the Nile River turning to blood, frogs overtaking the land, swarms of insects and flies, boils, locusts, and darkness throughout the land. Before the tenth plague, God instructs the Hebrews to protect themselves by preparing a special meal. They must slaughter a lamb and place the animal's blood above their doorways. The blood will signal the tenth plague to "pass over" the Hebrews.

As darkness falls, the firstborn male of every Egyptian household dies. The Hebrew people are spared with their Passover meal. Even Pharaoh's own son dies, so he orders the slaves out of Egypt. After four hundred years in Egypt, the Hebrew people numbering six hundred thousand men—plus their wives, children, and animals—leave. It's the first time the Hebrew people have acted together as a nation.

After they leave, Pharaoh changes his mind and wants his slave labor back. He sends his highest in command on chariots, and the Egyptians chase the Hebrews to the Red Sea. In one of the most spectacular acts of the Bible, the Lord parts the Red Sea to allow His people to cross. After they are safely on land, God allows the sea to return, killing all of Pharaoh's warriors.

As the group continues, they begin to grumble and complain about the lack of food and water. But just as God promised, He takes care of them. He provides water from a rock, and a substance called manna falls from the sky every morning, providing nourishment. The group camps at Mount Sinai, where God calls Moses to climb to the top. There, God gives Moses two tablets containing the Ten Commandments. These laws, along with very detailed instruction on how to build the sacrificial altar, the ark of the covenant, and the tabernacle, solidify the relationship and the promise between God and His chosen people. This covenant is a renewal of the original promise the Lord made to Abraham many years ago. The Hebrew people are now an Israelite nation.

Unfortunately the people continue to complain. They are led to the edge of the Promised Land of Canaan, which covers approximately the area of modern-day Israel. Spies are sent out ahead of the people to survey the land and inhabitants. The spies scare the Israelites with terrible stories of giants they could not possibly defeat. They refuse to enter Canaan, and as punishment, the Lord causes them to wander throughout the desert for forty years. During this time, a generation has died, and a renewed group of Israelites is ready to enter Canaan.

Moses is very old at this time and will die before entering Canaan. Joshua is put in charge of the conquest. Once again, spies are sent ahead to scout out the land. A prostitute, Rahab, lives in the city of Jericho in Canaan, and she assists the spies by hiding them from capture. In return, Rahab and her family are protected during the subsequent battle.

God instructs Joshua to march around the city for seven days, blow trumpets, and shout. With that, the walls of the city of Jericho come down. The entire city is burned, but Rahab's family is spared. Rahab is important to the story because she will go on to be the great-great grandmother of King David and an ancestor of Jesus Christ.

The Promised Land is called the Land of Milk and Honey because, just as God promised, it is good for grazing and bearing fruit trees. The land is divided into sections, forming twelve tribes named for the sons of Jacob.

DISCUSSION QUESTIONS

1. The Jewish people still celebrate the Passover meal today. Discuss the significance of this holiday.

2. The Lord gives the law in painstaking detail. His specific instruction allows a holy place for the Lord to commune with His people. What does this say about how God feels about His people?

3. Think about the purpose of the Ten Commandments, found in Exodus 20:1–17. Do these commandments make you think of God as a dictator? Instead think of the Ten Commandments as loving instruction to a child by a caring parent. The parent only wants what is best for the child. Now discuss your view of God in these terms.

4. What do you think about Rahab, a prostitute, being an ancestor to Christ?

TRIBES AND JUDGES

"IN THOSE DAYS, ISRAEL HAD NO KING; EVERYONE DID AS he saw fit" (Judges 21:25). In the opening of Judges, Joshua is dead, and the Israelites have not completely eradicated the former inhabitants of Canaan. Instead the Israelites begin to live among them, intermarrying and worshipping their idol gods. The term "judge" does not mean what it does in today's language. A judge in biblical times is more of a tribal leader.

The book of Judges records a series of cycles: Israelite sinning, suffering, calling out to the Lord, gaining forgiveness, and earning deliverance. This cycle happens over and over again.

The female judge Deborah is worth noting not only because she stands out as a woman in an all-man world, but because she was also a general commanding an army and a prophet. Deborah's enemy is the Canaanite, Sisera. Deborah begins a battle against Sisera, and when he runs and hides, Jael, another woman, kills him.

In another cycle of sin, the Midianites completely overtake the Israelites. The Midianites are like a plague to the Israelites. They steal their harvests and livestock and force the Israelites into caves and other hiding places away from the biblical bullies.

The Lord calls upon a young Israelite male, Gideon, to deliver

His people from this oppression. Gideon tries to argue with the angel of the Lord, telling the angel that he is the weakest member of the weakest family group. Still the angel of the Lord presses Gideon and promises to help him in battle. After Gideon tests the Lord and the Lord patiently allows His authenticity to be verified, Gideon finally trusts. With the Lord's help, Gideon's army is reduced to three hundred to clearly show God's hand in the work of defeating the Midian army. Upon the Lord's instruction, Gideon's small army surrounds the Midians. The Israelite army shouts and blows trumpets, and the Lord drives out the Midians, confusing them to fight each other to their deaths.

Another notable cycle of sin involves Samson. The enemy this time is the Philistines. Unlike the Midians, the Philistines are very close to the Israelites, almost friendly and with some intermarriage. God chooses Samson to possess enormous strength in the form of a one-man army … with one condition. Samson must not cut his hair.

The Israelites are still in the Bronze Age, using bronze weapons, whereas the Philistines have learned how to make iron weapons. So Samson promises to be a great advantage to the Israelite people. In one amazing act, Samson defeats an army of a thousand men with the jawbone of a donkey.

Samson's downfall is his love of women, and Delilah is particularly lethal. Delilah, a Philistine woman, nags him day after day as to the secret of his strength. Finally, tired of the agonizing, Samson tells her his secret.

So while Samson is asleep, Delilah has his head shaved, and the Philistines capture and blind him. They force Samson into slave labor. One day he is taken to the crowded temple, and in a prayer, Samson asks God for revenge. Leaning against the temple pillar, Samson exerts his last strength to bring down the temple, killing everyone, including himself.

The book of Ruth is included here because it takes places during the time of Judges. Judges illustrates the behavior of the people of Israel on a large scale, whereas Ruth gives us a glimpse into the lives of the common people at this time.

During a time of famine in Canaan, a man takes his wife Naomi and his two sons to the land of Moab, located east of Canaan. In Moab, the two sons marry local Moab women. One of these women is Ruth. Unfortunately, while the family lives in Moab, the father and both the sons die, leaving the women alone. Naomi urges the young widows to return to their mothers and find new husbands, but Ruth refuses to leave Naomi. Without family to care for her, Naomi begins the voyage home to Canaan with Ruth faithfully at her side.

Once back in Canaan, Naomi and Ruth work for a relative of Naomi's husband, Boaz. In biblical times, it was not only customary, but it was God's law for a widow to be given in marriage to a relative of her dead husband.

Boaz seems like the perfect husband for Ruth. With only a little persuasion on her part, Ruth is easily able to entice him into marriage. Boaz covers Ruth with his protection, and they have a son, Obed, who becomes the father of Jesse, who becomes the father of King David. This makes Ruth the great-grandmother of King David.

DISCUSSION

1. The cycle of sinning, suffering, forgiveness, and deliverance happens over and over again. The Israelites seem not to learn any lessons, yet God continues to forgive them when they call out to Him. What does this mean for your life?

2. Gideon tests the Lord's authenticity, and God is very patient with him. Does this reflect how you feel about someone you love?

3. Samson is blessed, yet he has a weakness for disreputable women, which is his ultimate downfall. Have you ever received a blessing but lost it to a bad decision?

4. Ruth is not an Israelite woman. She is a Moabite, an Arab. Why do you think God included her in the line to King David and Jesus Christ?

A UNIFIED NATION

SAMUEL IS ISRAEL'S LAST JUDGE, OR DELIVERER SENT from God. The story of Israel becoming a unified nation begins with First Samuel, whose author is unknown. The date is about 1100 BC and covers around one hundred years. Second Samuel and the beginning of First Kings also cover the unified nation era of Israel.

A barren woman, Hannah, calls out to God to be blessed with a son. In return, she promises to give the child back to God in service. Within a year, Hannah gives birth to a baby boy, Samuel. His mother dedicates him to the Lord when he is weaned and eating solid foods. An old priest, Eli, needs assistance, so Samuel is sent to live with him and to faithfully serve him. Samuel grows up as Eli's personal attendant.

At this time in history, the Israelites are at war with the Philistines. The Philistines arrive on the eastern coast of the Mediterranean at about the same time the Hebrew people are entering Canaan. The two groups are frequently campaigning war against each other.

In one particular siege, the Israelites foolishly decide to bring the ark of the covenant with them into battle. God did not tell the Israelites to bring the ark into battle. The ark of the covenant was basically a large box used to carry around the Ten Commandments, which Moses had received from the Lord. When Joshua first invaded the Promised Land, the presence of the ark of the covenant indicated God's presence and His leadership. For this reason, the people probably thought bringing the ark into battle was a good decision.

Unfortunately the battle ends in disaster. Eli's two sons are killed, and the Philistines capture the ark. Upon hearing this news, Eli, who is blind and elderly, falls backward and dies. Even the bride of one of Eli's deceased sons goes into labor, gives birth, and dies.

The Philistines consider the ark of the covenant a trophy of war. Soon however, in the city where the ark is kept, tumors plague the people. The Philistines move the ark to another city and then another, and still the plague spreads. Finally the ark is returned to the Israelites.

The nations surrounding the tribes of Israel all have kings at this time, and the people have begun to believe they also need a king to compete with their enemies. Samuel hears them calling out for a king. "And the Lord told him: 'Listen to all that the people are saying to you; it is not you they have rejected, but they have rejected me as their king" (1 Samuel 8:7).

Samuel anoints the first king of Israel, a donkey herder, Saul, who is reluctant for the job at first. But then he agrees to his position and becomes an accomplished leader. God is with Saul at first, but Saul begins to make unwise decisions, ignoring God's instructions. Soon God leaves Saul, and an evil spirit that torments Saul replaces God. The Lord rejects Saul as king and instructs Samuel to anoint David, a young sheepherder.

In one particular confrontation with the Philistines, an enormous Philistine, Goliath, presents himself before the battle and challenges any man who will fight him one on one to the death. The winner will win the battle for his own side. The young David, who is serving the men in Saul's army, steps forward to confront the giant.

Saul tries to talk him out of it, but David reassures Saul that he has killed lions before and the Lord is with him. David gathers smooth stones from the river for the battle, but he only needs one. With one stone, David knocks Goliath unconscious. David takes Goliath's iron sword and cuts off his head.

The women greet the heroes with a song that infuriates Saul. "As they danced, they sang, 'Saul has slain his thousands, and David his tens of thousands'" (1 Samuel 18:7). Now jealousy overcomes Saul, and David's life is in jeopardy. With the trusted friendship of Saul's son, Jonathan, David is able to run, hide, and elude Saul's attempts on his life. David even has occasion to kill Saul, but he refuses to kill God's anointed one. First Samuel ends in battle with Saul's sons dying and Saul taking his own life.

The author of Second Samuel is also unknown, as it was originally one book with First Samuel. In this book, the United Kingdom of Israel continues with the reign of King David.

A messenger returns from battle with the news of Saul's death. Then David asks the Lord where he should go, to which the Lord responded, "To Hebron." Hebron is the capital of Judah, the southern part of the kingdom. In Hebron, David is anointed king over Judah while Saul's surviving son, Ish-Bosheth, maintains command of the Northern Kingdom, Israel.

It's no surprise that what follows is an ongoing struggle between the two. And over time, "David grew stronger and stronger, while the house of Saul grew weaker and weaker" (2 Samuel 3:1). Eventually Ish-Bosheth is murdered, and David becomes king over Israel, the Northern Kingdom, as well.

King David is sent out to conquer the Jebusites, who inhabit an area between the Northern and Southern Kingdoms of Israel. The Lord is with David, and he successfully takes the land, making a capital, the city of David. The ark of the covenant is brought here. Many successful campaigns follow, including those against the Philistines, Moabites, Ammonites, and Edomites. David expands the kingdom and strengthens Israel with his many victories.

Things are going well for David on the battlefront. Unfortunately at home, David makes a decision that begins a downward spiral in his own life. One afternoon in the springtime, the men are away waging war, but David remains at home. He wakes up from a nap and watches a woman taking a bath on her rooftop. David summons Bathsheba, the woman who is the wife of Uriah, a man away in battle. He sleeps with her, and she becomes pregnant. So David sends word to Joab, the captain of his army, to send Uriah home in hopes he will sleep with his wife, absolving David of his transgression.

Regrettably the plan does not work because Uriah refuses to sleep with his wife while his fellow comrades are away. After sending Uriah back to the fighting, David tells Joab to send Uriah to the most dangerous area of the battle and then to leave him unprotected. Uriah dies, Bathsheba becomes King David's wife, and David is responsible for murder in the eyes of the Lord.

The Lord sends the prophet Nathan to rebuke David for his actions. David realizes his sins and asks for forgiveness, but the son of Bathsheba and David dies a few days after his birth.

Conditions in King David's house grow worse when his son Amnon rapes his half-sister Tamar. In retaliation, Tamar's full brother, Absalom, kills Amnon. Absalom flees and lives separate from his father for years. The king is torn over his feelings for his son. Eventually Absalom assembles trusted followers who meet David's men in battle. Joab ultimately kills Absalom, and King David is distraught.

Soon King David's wages of war fail as he grows tired with sin.

The Lord judges David, and a plague strikes all of Israel, killing seventy thousand people. "David built an altar to the Lord there and sacrificed burnt offerings and fellowship offerings. Then the Lord answered prayer in behalf of the land, and the plague on Israel was stopped" (2 Samuel 24:25).

First Kings opens with David old and on his deathbed. He declares Solomon, a son he later has with Bathsheba, to be the next king. Now Solomon has a big problem because he has sixteen older brothers ahead of him in line for the position of king. Fortunately the prophet and close advisor to King David favors Solomon as king.

When David dies and Solomon becomes king, the Lord appears to him in a dream and asks him, "What do you want?" Solomon chooses to ask for wisdom. And Solomon becomes most famous for his wisdom. Solomon writes three of the wisest and most beautiful poetic books of the Bible: Proverbs, Ecclesiastes, and Song of Songs.

Solomon rules over Israel during peacetime. Because his father has conquered many enemies in war before him, Solomon has the luxury of time to build a permanent temple in Jerusalem. The ark of the covenant is brought from the city of David to the new temple.

King Solomon loves many women, as he has seven hundred wives and three hundred mistresses. These women unfortunately turn out to be his downfall. Many of the wives are from lands of foreign neighbors who worship idols and false gods. Eventually Solomon begins participating in their idolatry rituals, displeasing the Lord.

Solomon reigns the United Kingdom of Israel for forty years. Upon his death in the 900s BC, the kingdom is divided and ruled by different kings.

DISCUSSION

1. The Israelites took matters into their own hands by bringing the ark of the covenant into battle without God's request to do so. When have you tried to control matters of your own life without God's input? And how did things turn out?

2. As Israel calls out for a king, God allows it, knowing it is the wrong choice. Why do you think God allowed them this choice? And why do you think He allows us to make mistakes in our lives?

3. Saul is good at first, serving God. His initial sins against God are very subtle, but they grow quickly to murderous intentions. Saul slipped from God from very quickly. In what ways have you observed this in your life or someone you know?

4. King David did well in battle, but his home life was falling apart. What does this say about how we should handle our own lives?

5. If the Lord appeared to you in a dream and asked you what you would want, what would you ask for?

6. Solomon's wives brought him down. Has a person or group of people ever caused you to stray from God and what you knew was right?

A NATION DIVIDED

FIRST AND SECOND KINGS TELL THE HISTORY OF THE mostly unrighteous kings of Israel and Judah after Solomon's death. First and Second Chronicles recount almost the same material but from a different perspective. The divided nation covers the time period from about 930 until 586 BC.

Rehoboam, son of Solomon, rules the Southern Kingdom called Judah. Judah actually consists of two of the original twelve tribes of Israel, Judah and Benjamin. Jeroboam, a former associate of King Solomon, rules the Northern Kingdom. The Northern Kingdom rules the remaining ten tribes of Israel.

A long line of disobedient kings follow Rehoboam and Jeroboam in both kingdoms. The kings' biggest sin is their idol worship and reverence for terrible false gods such as Baal and Molech. They build altars and temples to these idols, and they seem to have forgotten their covenant with the Lord who promised protection and blessings in return for obedience.

God sends prophets during this time to warn the leaders and help the people of Israel. Elijah, Elisha, Obadiah, and Isaiah are some of the prophets sent to counsel the chosen people and serve the Lord. Elijah is sent to warn the officials and kings about their sin of idolatry and the consequences. Elisha succeeds Elijah and ministers to the common people, healing and performing miracles. Obadiah hides a hundred of the Lord's prophets in two caves so he can save them from execution by Queen Jezebel. Isaiah accurately predicts the exile of the Israelite people.

The Lord sends the prophet Elijah to visit the Northern King Ahab and his Queen Jezebel. This couple is particularly evil in the Lord's eyes. They worship Baal, and the queen kills the Lord's prophets. After killing Naboth for his vineyard, Elijah tells them the Lord will kill them both for their sin and their bodies will be eaten by dogs and vultures. And this is precisely what happens.

The last leader of the Northern Kingdom, King Hoshea, stops paying the taxes imposed by a neighboring oppressive group, the Assyrians. And in 722 BC, King Shalmaneser of Assyria captures the Northern Kingdom and Israelite people. Some Israelites die, others are exiled, and many escape and remain among the new settlers in the land that was once Israel. Interestingly the Israelites who remain in Israel integrate themselves with foreign people, marry them, and, generations later, create a race known as the Samaritans.

However, amidst this dark period, a few righteous kings emerge in the Southern Kingdom. In 715 BC, the Assyrian Empire attempts to conquer King Hezekiah of the Southern Kingdom of Judah. King Sennacherib of Assyria decides to invade Judah when King Hezekiah refuses to be bullied with taxation. King Sennacherib and his warriors drive the king and his people inside the walls of Jerusalem. As everyone slept "that night the angel of the Lord went out and put to death a hundred and eighty-five thousand men in the Assyrian camp. When the people got up the next morning—there were all the dead bodies!" (2 Kings 19:35).

The prophet Isaiah, who has been held up in the city of Jerusalem, accurately predicts that King Sennacherib would "return by the way you came" (2 Kings 19:28). And the king of Assyria does indeed go home by the way he came.

After the fall of the Northern Kingdom to the Assyrians in 722 BC, the Babylonians conquer the Assyrians in 612 BC.

As the Southern Kingdom of Judah continues to struggle with sinful, unrighteous kings, they hold out until 586 BC when King Nebuchadnezzar II of Babylonia surrounds the city of Jerusalem and starves the people into surrender. The nation of Israel no longer exists, and God's chosen people are in exile.

Second Chronicles ends with Cyrus, the Persian king, conquering Babylonia about fifty years after the fall of Jerusalem. Cyrus announces he is letting the Jewish people go and return to Jerusalem after a total of seventy years in exile.

DISCUSSION

1. God sent many prophets during the era of the divided kingdom, but no one listened. Have you had the experience of God's love trying to reach you during a time when you were unable or unwilling to listen?

2. The ungodly kings of both kingdoms worshipped false gods. This may be a sin you feel you can safely exclude from your own personal list of sins. But consider the modern-day worship of money, power, and materialism. How do these idols contribute to our personal downfall? How does this kind of worship affect those closest to us?

3. The Samaritans became an unaccepted race in the New Testament. They are considered impure because they are a mix of Israelites and foreign settlers. Thousands of years later, we still label certain groups of people negatively. Do you think this disrespects God?

4. After so many years of sin, punishment, and exile, the Jewish people were still God's chosen people. The covenant still stood. Think for a moment about the patience God has for His people. Think about how more meaningful your life could be if you believed with all your heart that you are loved by a God this patient with you.

EXILE ERA

THE BIBLE SEEMS TO SKIP THE SEVENTY YEARS GOD'S chosen people spend in exile. This is a good example you'll find where the Bible is not in chronological order. To read about the time the Hebrew people live in exile, we skip to the prophetical books of Ezekiel and Daniel.

Before the Babylonians finally take down Jerusalem in 586 BC, they have made two previous visits to the Israelites. In 605 BC, after Babylon conquers Assyria, they come as a sort of a "meet and greet" to introduce themselves as the new bully in town and to request taxation. In 597 BC, on their second visit, the Babylonians come to collect these taxes when the king refuses to pay. This time, thousands of Jewish people are taken back to Babylon. Ezekiel is taken at this time.

In Israel, Ezekiel is a priest, but in Babylon, the Lord visits him and makes him a prophet for the people in exile. God has two messages for His people:

1. The first is more of a notification that they would be completely destroyed in the crush of Jerusalem in 586 BC. This will be the punishment for years of disobedience.
2. The second is that He will allow His chosen people to be restored.

Ezekiel is sent to warn and reassure the people that Jerusalem will eventually be rebuilt. A particularly interesting prophesy is found in Ezekiel 37, the Valley of Dry Bones. The prediction is an analogy of the Hebrew people. Ezekiel's vision is of dry bones in a valley snapping together. "I will attach tendons to you and make flesh come upon you with skin; I will put breath in you, and you will come to life. Then you will know that I am the Lord" (Ezekiel 37:6). God will eventually restore His people.

The book of Daniel recounts the life of a young Israelite prince taken in exile by King Nebuchadnezzar II. Daniel is appointed an apprentice position in Babylon, along with three other young Hebrew exiles, Shadrach, Meshach, and Abednego. Daniel is more than a prophet in exile. He is also a dream interpreter, and in doing so, he becomes a close advisor to the king.

The king erects a huge golden idol for his top officials to worship, and everyone is commanded to bow in reverence to the statue. Shadrach, Meshach, and Abednego refuse. When the king confronts them, they steadfastly refuse to worship a false god. The king orders them to be thrown into a fiery furnace used as a kiln.

To the king's amazement, he looks into the furnace and sees the Lord inside with them. "Look! I see four men walking around in the fire, unbound and unharmed, and the fourth looks like a son of the gods" (Daniel 3:25). The king orders them freed and praises the God of Shadrach, Meshach, and Abednego and decrees that no one shall say anything against their God.

Years later, the last king of Babylonia, King Belshazzar, is having a party as the Persian Empire is closing in. The year is 539 BC, and during the party, the hand of God begins writing on the wall of the royal palace, "This is the inscription that was written: MENE, MENE, TEKEL, PARSIN" (Daniel 5:25). It means "numbered, numbered, weighed, divided." Selfish, idol-worshiping King Belshazzar days of reign are numbered. He has been found lacking, and his kingdom will be destroyed. That night, the Persians conquer Babylon and kill the king.

King Cyrus is the king of the Persian Empire with Darius of Medes, who is probably a regional leader. Under Darius, Daniel continues his place of prominence among the officials, and Darius shows him favor. Other officials become jealous of Daniel and plot to have him killed. Daniel is caught praying to his God, and Darius reluctantly orders him to the lion's den. Darius cannot sleep all night.

In the morning, Darius is relieved to hear Daniel shout to him, proclaiming that his God had shut the lion's mouths. Daniel is rescued and "prospered during the reign of Darius and the reign of Cyrus the Persian" (Daniel 6:28).

DISCUSSION

1. God speaks through Ezekiel to let the Hebrew people know they will be punished and then later restored. How does this reflect the behavior of a responsible earthly father?

2. Read Ezekiel 37:1–14. God has the power to restore something thought to be dead, a hopeless situation. Discuss a time when God did something in your life that you considered impossible.

3. The faith of Daniel, Meshach, Shadrach, and Abednego faces the ultimate test. What would it take for you to demonstrate this kind of faith?

4. King Belshazzar decides to throw a party, as he is about to be conquered and killed. When things seem most hopeless in your life, do you pray and focus on your next best step in life, or do you tend turn to temporary vices that can hurt you?

RETURN FROM EXILE

EZRA, NEHEMIAH, AND ESTHER ARE THE THREE BIBLICAL books set during the time after the Israelites are allowed to return to Jerusalem in Judah. These books together are akin to one story with a surprise twist at the end.

In 538 BC, more than forty-two thousand Jewish men return to Judah in accordance to the words of King Cyrus of Persia. Not only does the king release them, he also helps them by returning many of the items stolen by the Babylonians during the destruction of Jerusalem. Interestingly, not everyone leaves, and not all Jewish people leave at one time. Some stay behind because, after seventy years, it is the only home they know.

After the returned exiles settle in the land of Judah, they go to work on the temple. The foreigners who had made their homes there are not happy. They attempt to stop work on the temple by appealing to the king of Persia, but eventually the Jewish people are approved to finish. And the temple is complete in 515 BC.

Ezra the priest is part of a second wave who returns to Jerusalem in 458 BC. Ezra goes to the temple to pray and begins crying out to God because he fears the Jewish people have fallen back into sin. Shecaniah convinces Ezra to order all Israelite men to divorce their foreign wives and turn them away. Because of the sin King Solomon brought on by marrying foreign women, the instruction to the men is meant as a rejection of sin. Jewish law does not require a divorce on these grounds, and in fact, King David's great-grandmother Ruth was not an Israelite woman. Scholars find this decision by Ezra interesting and odd.

In 445 BC, Nehemiah is a Jewish cupbearer to King Artaxerxes of Persia. As the king's wine taster, Nehemiah holds a special place in the kingdom. Nehemiah and the king are close and possibly friends. Nehemiah's brother returns from Jerusalem to tell him that the wall around the temple city is destroyed and in ruins. When Nehemiah asks the king to allow him to go to Judah to rebuild the wall, the king is happy to permit him leave.

Once in Jerusalem, Nehemiah finds opposition from the foreign settlers in the area. They are concerned that the wall represents domination over them, and it is seen as a threat. So fearful of the rebuilding, the foreigners threaten violence and even plot to kill Nehemiah. Fortunately Nehemiah is wise to them and avoids being killed.

Nehemiah writes, "They were all trying to frighten us, thinking, 'their hands will get too weak for the work, and it will not be completed.' But I prayed, 'Now strengthen my hands'" (Nehemiah 6:9).

Determined to finish the wall, Nehemiah assigns teams to various sections of the wall. The men take turns working and standing guard. The wall is finished in an astonishing fifty-two days. The Jewish people are reunited in the temple and worship once again as a unified people. The priest Ezra reads from the law of Moses, and this is a time of great celebration and renewal.

The book of Esther features a young, beautiful Jewish girl who won the heart of King Xerxes of Persia. A yearlong beauty competition takes place in the kingdom for all the maidens. Before the year is over, the king shows increased interest in Esther. The king has many women in his harem, but he chooses Esther to wear the crown of queen. The king knows nothing of her Jewish identity.

Esther is an orphan raised by her cousin Mordecai, who also happens to work in the king's palace. Trouble starts when Mordecai refuses to bow to one of the king's noblemen, Haman. Haman asks why he does not bow, and Mordecai simply tells him that he is Jewish.

Enraged, Haman ponders his next step. Should he kill Mordecai? No, Haman believes it better to get rid of all the Jewish people because they threaten the authority of the king.

Haman tells the king that a group of people in Persia are a threat and must be annihilated. Not knowing the details, King Xerxes issues a decree ordering the holocaust. Haman decides on a date for the killing to begin by casting lots, or the Hebrew word *pur*. The date is one year away, giving time for the word to spread throughout the Persian kingdom.

A terrified Mordecai convinces young Esther to talk to her husband and reveal her identity. Esther is afraid for her life, but she agrees. When she approaches the king, he is happy to see her. So she invites him to a private banquet—just the king, herself, and Haman. Courageously, she tells the king her identity and says that someone has arranged to kill her and all her family.

An enraged King Xerxes asks who it is, and she points to Haman and says it is him. The king decides Haman should be executed. And ironically Haman is hanged on the same pole he had meant for the execution of Mordecai.

Unfortunately the king cannot reverse his decree, but he does issue a new one that allows the Jewish people to defend themselves and to take the property of those who try to harm them.

The upper nobles and officials support King Xerxes as the day draws near. On the intended day, all ten of Haman's sons are killed during a lengthy battle. The Jewish people survive, and the holocaust is avoided. The date is March 7, 473 BC, several years before Ezra and Nehemiah left Persia for Jerusalem.

Today the Jewish people still celebrate the courage of Esther with the holiday known as Purim.

DISCUSSION

1. It must have been a hard decision for Ezra to make concerning the divorce of so many fellow Jews. What decisions have you had to make in life where neither choice seemed best?

2. Nehemiah and his teams completed the wall around the temple city of Jerusalem in fifty-two days. Have you had the experience of doing your best work under pressure? In what ways at work or in other areas have you worked as a team with others and achieved more than you ever thought you could?

3. King Xerxes seems to truly love Esther. Esther was terrified because the king could put anyone to death on his order, even her. But she bravely went before him, telling him everything. God plants seeds in us for His purpose. Seeds of love and courage are used to save God's chosen people, his original covenant beginning with Abraham. In what ways does God use you and your heart for His purpose?

FIVE BOOKS OF POETRY

WE HAVE COME TO THE FIVE BOOKS OF POETRY IN THE Bible: Job, Psalms, Proverbs, Ecclesiastes, and Song of Songs (also known as Song of Solomon.) These books are set in earlier time periods of the Bible, so they do not follow chronological order.

Job is set all the way back during the time of Genesis, and the author is unknown. Job is a good man who is rich in livestock, children, and health. Satan notices Job and asks God's permission to take away Job's wealth as a test of his faith. Satan believes Job will curse God. God disagrees and allows the test.

All of Job's livestock and his ten children are killed. And then painful skin eruptions plague Job. Job's wife and friends encourage him to confess an unknown sin he must have committed to incur this punishment. Job refuses to repent for something he hasn't done.

Finally Job asks God why He has caused this destruction in his life. God answers only that everything under heaven belongs to Him and Job learns to simply trust God. Eventually God restores all of Job's wealth—both his health and livestock—and he has another ten children. The book of Job is the answer to why bad things happen to good people.

"The Lord is my shepherd, I shall not want. He makes me lie

down in green pastures, he leads me besides quiet waters, he restores my soul. He guides me in paths of righteousness for his name's sake" (Psalm 23:1–3). The book of Psalms is a collection of Hebrew verses gathered over a long period of time. About half of the psalms are credited to King David, which is set during 2 Samuel. Other authors are King Solomon, Moses, Asaph, and Ethan, and these are set during the corresponding time periods of history. Some of the psalms do not have a writer credited to them. Many of these verses are meant to be set to music, and for centuries they have been used for Jewish religious ceremonies and festivals.

King Solomon is author of the book of Proverbs, and it is set during First Kings. Proverbs is a collection of wise sayings that are generally good advice about staying out of trouble. "The fear of the Lord is the beginning of knowledge, but fools despise wisdom and discipline" (Proverbs 1:7). Instruction in this book includes a wide variety of topics—from raising children, working out conflicts with others, and respecting the role of wives to providing advice about the consequences of adultery.

Ecclesiastes, another book by King Solomon, teaches that everything of this world is meaningless without God. "'Meaningless! Meaningless!' says the Teacher. 'Utterly meaningless! Everything is meaningless!'" (Ecclesiastes 1:2). This book has a dark tone, and some speculate King Solomon wrote it toward the end of his life when his foreign wives had led him astray with false idols.

Song of Songs, another book by King Solomon, is a beautiful love story narrating the intimate love between the king and his Shulamite bride. In this book, married love and passion is celebrated and described in detail.

DISCUSSION

1. Think about a time when you felt like Job. What were your thoughts and feelings about God at this time? How did you handle your situation? Did you pray or ask God why?

2. Read Psalms 91. This chapter is a prayer for protection. Sometimes our own situations in life may seem frightening. By stepping back and putting God in control, only then can we truly feel His divine protection. Discuss these situations in your own lives.

3. "Train a child in the way he should go, and when he is old he will not turn from it" (Proverbs 22:6). Do you agree with this verse?

4. Read Ecclesiastes 3. Discuss God's perfect plan and the timing of all things. Include nature, relationships, work, and world events in your discussion.

5. Song of Songs, which quotes two lovers, seems out of place in the Bible. Why do you think it was included?

THE PROPHETS

PROPHETICAL LITERATURE IS FOUND IN THE FINAL SECTION
of the Old Testament. The last seventeen books of the Old Testament
consist of five major prophetical books and twelve minor prophetical
books. The major prophets are only called major because they are
longer books and we know more about them. Likewise, the minor
prophets are shorter books; therefore, we know less about these
prophets.

I won't go into too much detail about each of these books, but I
will touch on each one, orienting you to the time period, which group
the prophets are ministering to, and any interesting or outstanding
facts.

MAJOR PROPHETICAL BOOKS
- Isaiah
- Jeremiah
- Lamentations
- Ezekiel
- Daniel

MINOR PROPHETICAL BOOKS

- Hosea
- Joel
- Amos
- Obadiah
- Jonah
- Micah
- Nahum
- Habakkuk
- Zephaniah
- Haggai
- Zechariah
- Malachi

Isaiah is the first major prophetical book, ministering mainly to Judah, the Southern Kingdom about 740 to 700 BC. Isaiah also predicts the nation will be restored. Isaiah 7:14 says, "Therefore the Lord himself will give you a sign: The virgin will be with child and will give birth to a son, and will call him Immanuel." Isaiah foretells the birth of Jesus.

Jeremiah ministered from 627 to 586 BC. He prophesies that Jerusalem and Judah will fall to the Babylonians, but it will also be restored seventy years later. Jeremiah witnesses and lives through the attack.

An unknown author wrote Lamentations. The time period covered from 588 to 586 BC is an era of great suffering, sadness, and despair. The Babylonians surround the city and starve the people for two and a half years. The desperation in this book reflects their questions about whether or not they are still God's chosen people.

Ezekiel and Daniel are the final two major prophets who were already covered in the Exile Era section.

Hosea is the first minor book of the Bible. Hosea ministers to the Northern Kingdom of Israel from 750 to 722 BC. Strangely, God orders Hosea to marry a prostitute, Gomer. Soon Gomer runs back to her former life, and God tells Hosea to buy her back and bring her home. Hosea obeys God. God is illustrating how He loves Israel. Even though Israel has "prostituted" itself through idol worship, God still loves them, will buy them back, and bring them home.

Joel's message occurs about 750 BC. Israel is urged to repent, or it will be swarmed like a plague of locusts. Joel warns the locusts will be like soldiers; in fact they will be soldiers of the Assyrian army in 722 BC when the Northern Kingdom is destroyed.

Amos is a poor shepherd living in the Southern Kingdom of Judah in the mid-700s BC. God tells Amos to travel to the Northern Kingdom of Israel to warn them of their sinful ways. The book of Amos is uncommon because he is the first commoner to be called upon by God to deliver a message as a prophet.

Obadiah is unique in that it's a message to the nation of Edom, a land just southeast of the former nation of Judah. After the fall of Jerusalem in 586 BC, Obadiah tells the people of Edom that God will punish them for killing Israeli refugees as they fled from the Babylonian destruction.

Jonah is a rebellious prophet. He lived about 750 BC, and his prophecy is the only one that did not turn out as expected. God instructs Jonah to travel to Nineveh, the capital of Assyria, and tell the people that God will destroy them in forty days. Jonah refuses, and after spending three days and nights in the belly of a big fish, he decides to deliver the message for God. The people of Nineveh hear the prophecy and repent, and God does not destroy them. Jonah ends up probably disappointed that God didn't judge and destroy the people of Nineveh, whom he hated.

Micah, like Amos, is a poor villager who ministers to the rich, higher class, dishonest men of Judah. In 742 BC, Micah foretells the destruction of the Northern and Southern Kingdoms, the exile of the survivors, and the eventual restoration of the Jews to their homeland.

Nahum, like Jonah, is instructed by God to minister to Nineveh in Assyria. In the mid-600s BC, the northern nation of Israel has already been captured by Assyria, but the southern nation of Judah remains intact. God's message through Nahum to the Assyrian people is that they will be destroyed for their sins of idolatry. Babylonia conquers them in 612 BC.

Habakkuk is set between the fall of Assyria and the fall of Jerusalem in 586 BC. Habakkuk is upset by the sin, violence, and disobedience of the people, and he prays to God, asking why He doesn't stop it. God answers that He will send the Babylonians to destroy Jerusalem and the sin.

Zephaniah ministers in 640 BC. The message from God is that this is His very last warning for the people to repent before Jerusalem is destroyed.

Haggai ministers in 520 BC. He is the first of three post-exile prophets. In 539 BC, the first Jews are allowed to return to Jerusalem and rebuild the temple. But eighteen years later, the temple is still lying in ruins. The message was to finish rebuilding the temple.

Zechariah ministers from 520 to 518 BC. The second post-exile prophet, he reassures the workers of the temple that God is watching over them. Zechariah also foretells of the coming Messiah.

Malachi ministers in the 400s BC. The third and final post-exile prophet, Malachi warns that God is displeased with sins that are creeping in. People are sacrificing defective offerings, not tithing one-tenth to the temple, and marrying foreign women. Obedience is emphasized in Malachi, and the book ends with God's promise of a coming Messiah. "See, I will send my messenger, who will prepare the way before me. Then suddenly the Lord you are seeking will come to his temple; the messenger of the covenant, whom you desire, will come," says the Lord Almighty" (Malachi 3:1).

In this verse, Malachi is foretelling the one who will pave the way for the coming Lord. The Jewish people of today believe the Lord was speaking of Elijah. "See, I will send you the prophet Elijah" (Malachi 4:5). But Christians believe the one to pave the way for the Messiah was John the Baptist.

DISCUSSION

1. Jonah certainly didn't like his assignment from God. How do you think it felt to be a prophet in biblical times? Do you think it was dangerous or scary or a place of honor to be chosen by God?

2. God uses all types of people as prophets—willing and unwilling, rich and poor, or royalty and shepherds. What can we learn about the types of people God uses to deliver His messages?

3. False prophets were a problem in biblical times. They spoke from themselves rather than God. They said what people wanted to hear. We see this today in a variety of ways—infomercials, exuberant salesmen, and false advertisements. In what ways have today's false prophets taken advantage of you?

4. God is giving his chosen people many chances, several messages, and warnings to change their ways. Discuss a time in your own life when you were given a fair warning before a disaster but chose to ignore the red flags.

SILENCE ERA

MALACHI IS THE LAST WE HEAR FROM GOD FOR FOUR
hundred years. God goes silent during this time, but He remains at
work behind the scenes, and He is setting the stage for the birth of Jesus.

The Persian Empire is the ruling government at the close of the
Old Testament. During the silence, the Greeks, led by Alexander
the Great, conquer the Persians in 333 BC. Nearly two hundred
years later, the Romans destroy the Greek city of Corinth in 146 BC,
making Rome the new ruler in the region. The huge Roman Empire
brings peaceful times to the land, which encourages growth. The
Romans promote travel and communication by making roads and
unifying a common language throughout the region.

Under Roman rule, two religious sects govern the people of
Jerusalem. The Pharisees are a conservative group; the Sadducees
are a more liberal group. The two sit on a ruling board called the
Sanhedrin. The religious parties and Roman government oppress the
Jews during this time, treating them poorly.

During this time, the persecuted Jewish people are waiting for a
Savior. The Jews interpret the promised Savior as a physical king, a new
Roman ruler perhaps that will deliver them from political oppression.
They do not expect what will come next, a Messiah, the Son of God.

DISCUSSION

1. The silent years must have been devastating for the Jewish people. They worked and waited for the coming Savior. For four hundred years, generation after generation passed, and it seemed as though God had forgotten them. Have you ever prayed or called out to God and felt as though He doesn't hear you? How did your situation turn out? Do you think God was working behind the scenes on behalf of you and possibly a greater good that you could not understand at the time?

2. Expecting a Jewish leader who would become king and overthrow the Roman Empire, how do you think the people of this time felt when Jesus told them His was the kingdom of heaven?

3. God waits four hundred years to make sure everything is set for the arrival of His Son Jesus. He doesn't send His Son sooner. God waits until the right moment. Do you ever rush God's plan in your own life? Or have you ever waited too long to act on something? Discuss what you can learn from God's divine planning.

THE NEW
TESTAMENT

THE GOSPELS

EVERY PERSON, STORY, AND PROPHET IN THE OLD
Testament of the Bible points straight to the coming Messiah, Jesus,
the son of Mary and Joseph. The Gospels depict the birth, life, death,
and resurrection of the Messiah as prophesized in the Old Testament.
God sent His Son Jesus Christ to earth to die for our sins. His death
on the cross paid the price for the sins of all mankind forever. The
Jews—and every person for that matter—no longer needed to sacrifice
animals as offerings to make things right with God. The Lamb of God
was God's gift to us, a final sacrificial lamb.

The New Testament contains four gospels: Matthew, Mark,
Luke, and John. The Gospels give us four different points of view,
four different witnesses who emphasize different aspects. The word
"gospel" means good news, and the four gospels certainly deliver
good news to all people of the world. Matthew, Mark, and Luke
are known as synoptic gospels, meaning they are from a common
viewpoint. They all give similar, sometimes overlapping, accounts of
the birth, life, death, and resurrection of Jesus Christ, the Messiah.

The book of John is a bit different. John omits much material
found in the synoptic gospels, and most of the material in John is
not found in any other gospel. He does not include any parables at

all, and many of the miracles performed by Jesus are not in any other gospel. Most important, however, is the preaching genre that provides the reader with not merely a description of action, but a deeper, more reflective meaning.

During the ministry and travels of Jesus, He calls twelve men to follow Him. These twelve are known as disciples or apostles. Generally speaking, the word "disciple" is used while Jesus is living and teaching the men. The men are students, and Jesus is their teacher. The word "apostle" is a broader term used for a person who is sent for a purpose, or a mission.

The disciples are usually referred to as apostles after Jesus's death and after He sent them into the world to spread the good news. In the New Testament, the word "apostle" is sometimes used specifically for the twelve followers of Jesus and oftentimes used in the broader sense as a person on a mission for Christ.

THE GOSPEL OF MATTHEW

MATTHEW WAS NOT THE FIRST GOSPEL WRITTEN, BUT IT was likely chosen to be the first book of the New Testament because it is a natural bridge between the Old and New Testaments. Christ's disciple, Matthew the tax collector, is the writer, and he probably wrote it around AD 70. The date is disputed because Jesus foretells the destruction of the temple in AD 70. So it is not clear if the temple hadn't been destroyed yet or if had already happened, and that's why the prophecy is pointed out in the book.

The book of Matthew wants to show the Jews that Jesus is indeed the Messiah prophesized in the Old Testament. He begins with a lineage, Abraham through King David, through Jesus's earthly father, Joseph.

Matthew begins with a young virgin named Mary becoming pregnant through the Holy Spirit. A man named Joseph is promised to her in marriage but has second thoughts when he finds out she is pregnant. An angel of the Lord changes his mind, and he marries her. The two travel to Bethlehem in Judea, where Jesus is born. The year Jesus was born is disputed among scholars, but it is likely between 7 to 4 BC. Jesus is born during the reign of the jealous King Herod the Great.

Foreigners, men looking for the newborn king so they can worship Him, soon visit King Herod. The men find no newborn son in the kingdom. King Herod decides to use them to find out where the new king has been born. They find Jesus, worship Him, and bring gifts, but they go home a different way, avoiding King Herod. They are warned in a dream not to return to King Herod to tell him about the baby. Not knowing the location of the baby, King Herod decrees that all male babies ages two and under be killed to protect his own kingship. Joseph, Mary, and Jesus flee to Egypt for a short time until King Herod the Great dies in 4 BC. The family then returns home and settles in Nazareth.

In all of the gospels, Jesus's childhood is largely skipped over. In Matthew, we are now introduced to John the Baptist, who is baptizing people in the Jordan River when Jesus comes to be baptized. John thinks this is odd and says it is Jesus who should be baptizing him. John consents when Jesus says, "It is proper for us to do this to fulfill all righteousness" (Matthew 3:15). After Jesus is baptized, the Spirit of God says, "This is my Son, whom I love; with him I am well pleased" (Matthew 3:17).

After His baptism, Satan promises Jesus an earthly kingdom in exchange for His worship. For forty days and nights, Jesus is tested. Jesus simply tells Satan to leave, and angels of the Lord come to comfort him.

After the test, Jesus formally begins His ministry. He travels from Nazareth to Capernaum, where He begins calling His disciples. Simon (Peter) and his brother Andrew are fishermen called by Jesus. James and his younger brother John are also fishermen. The four men stop working (literally drop what they are doing) to follow Jesus.

Capernaum is in the region of Galilee where Jesus begins teaching in the synagogues. He heals the sick, dying, and paralyzed. He casts out evil spirits from those possessed by demons. Jesus begins performing miracles, and crowds start to follow Him.

Beginning in Matthew 5, Jesus sits down on a mountainside and gives a long lesson known as the Sermon on the Mount. Instruction ranges from loving your enemies to engaging in prayer, forbidding murder, and prohibiting adultery. The teaching also includes the famous beatitudes, which is radical thinking for the time. Jesus teaches them that those who are meek, poor, and persecuted will ultimately be in God's favor. This idea is new because, until then, only those with political power and authority were considered worthy of receiving wealth and riches. He also teaches them how to pray to God with a personal address of "Father" in the Lord's Prayer.

Jesus continues to preach and heal people along the way. Peter's mother-in-law is healed, along with a centurion's servant and even a girl thought to be dead. Soon his actions catch the attention of the Pharisees and Sadducees, who begin to taunt Him.

Jesus calls the rest of his disciples and gives them the ability to drive out demons and heal as well. Matthew, Philip, Bartholomew, Thomas, James (son of Alphacus), Thaddaeus, Simon the zealot, and Judas Iscariot were called in addition to the first four for a total of twelve disciples. He instructs them to go to the lost sheep of Israel.

As Jesus continues His teaching, He often speaks in parables, fictional stories used to illustrate a point. The parables are clever and often trip up even the disciples.

The Pharisees increasingly pick on Jesus when He would do things they perceive as against Jewish law. Jesus is accused of healing and working on the Sabbath, and He is asked several times for a miraculous sign from God. The pressure and hatred from the more conservative Pharisees is mounting.

Meanwhile Antipas, the son of King Herod the Great, imprisons

John the Baptist for attempting to correct the king on a moral matter. The king has been sleeping with his brother's wife and wants to continue to do so without interference from John. John learns from prison that Jesus is in fact the Messiah, and eventually Antipas beheads John during a party at the king's palace. John the Baptist was Jesus's cousin and friend; he was also the prophet who fulfilled the prophecies of Elijah's announcement of the Messiah's arrival.

Jesus and the disciples walk to Caesarea Philippi. Here, Jesus asks His disciples, "Who do people say the Son of Man is?" (Matthew 16:13). The disciples give their guesses: John the Baptist, Elijah, Jeremiah, or another prophet. Then Jesus turns to Simon Peter and asks him, "Who do you say I am?"(Matthew 16:15). Simon Peter confesses the answer, "You are the Christ, Son of the Living God" (Matthew 16:16).

Jesus blesses him for knowing the right answer, like many rabbis do when their students answer correctly. Amazingly Jesus tells Peter, "And I tell you that you are my Peter, and on this rock I will build my church" (Matthew 16:18).

After Jesus predicts his own suffering, death, and resurrection, He announces He will need to travel to Jerusalem. Six days later, Jesus takes three of his disciples—John, Peter, and James—with Him to a mountaintop. Here, Jesus transforms into a glowing white deity and speaks with Moses and Elijah. The disciples are in awe and realize that John the Baptist was Elijah.

Jesus and His disciples continue with large crowds following them. Jesus tells parables and performs miracles as before, but the pressure from the Pharisees escalates. They ask Him questions, attempting to trip Him up, but it never works, leaving the Pharisees looking like fools.

Finally Jesus enters Jerusalem, where He knows He will be put to death. He enters on a donkey, as prophesized, with palm leaves laid out before him. Entering Jerusalem marks the day known as Palm Sunday, the Sunday before Easter.

Once in Jerusalem, Jesus enters the temple and becomes enraged when He sees thieves using the house of prayer to sell their items. He overturns the tables and benches of those making money. He then teaches in the temple courts as the Pharisees continue to harass him. After speaking, Jesus leaves the temple and predicts it will be destroyed. He also foretells the end of times, although acknowledging that only God knows the date and hour when this will occur.

In the days before the Jewish celebration of Passover, the chief priests begin to plot against Jesus, deciding to arrest and kill Him in a deceptive way. Jesus knew of this plot through his divinity. One of Jesus's own disciples, Judas Iscariot, goes to the chief priest and agrees to hand Jesus over to them for a price of thirty silver coins.

Jesus instructs his disciples to prepare the Passover meal, a seder, a day early. The disciples do as they are told, and as Jesus sits together with the twelve, He tells them that one of them will betray Him. When Judas asks if it is him, Jesus answers it is. Judas then leaves the supper.

Then Jesus breaks bread with His disciples, blesses it, and explains it is His body. They drink from a cup He blesses, and Jesus tells them that this is His blood poured out for them. At the Lord's Supper, Jesus also predicts Peter will deny knowing Him three times before the rooster crows in the morning. Peter is astonished and attempts to reassure Jesus that he will never disown Him.

After they eat, the men go to Gethsemane, where the disciples sleep and Jesus prays. Jesus is apprehensive concerning His impending fate. He asks God to take away the burden if it is His will to do so. Then Judas arrives with the chief priests and elders and tells them to arrest the one he kisses. Jesus, betrayed by Judas's kiss, is arrested and taken to the home of Caiaphas, the high priest.

This gathering of the Sanhedrin discusses the situation, looking for false evidence against Him. Finally they decide He is guilty of blasphemy. The Sanhedrin, however, cannot put Him to death. Only a Roman official under Emperor Tiberius Caesar is authorized to execute a criminal.

Jesus is taken before Pontius Pilate, the Roman regional governor of Judea. Pilate is unable to find any reason to convict Jesus until He says He is King of the Jews. This statement becomes the false evidence they can use to put Jesus to death because proclaiming oneself as king is against Roman law.

Still uneasy about the decision, Pilate asks the crowd to decide. The crowd yells that they want Jesus crucified. Upon the crowd's decision, Pilate washes his hands in a basin (washing his hands of this responsibility) and says that this man's blood is not on his hands. Once Judas realizes what he has done, he feels remorse, returns the silver to the high priests, and hangs himself.

Jesus is mocked and tortured, and He is forced to carry His own cross to the place where He will be crucified. Hours pass, and Jesus hangs from the cross, dying. It is daytime, but a strange darkness falls over the land. The moment Jesus dies, an earthquake shakes Jerusalem. The temple curtain tears in half, and dead holy people rise back to life and walk among the people. Many people watch, and when evening comes, Joseph of Arimathea asks Pilate for the body of Jesus. Pilate agrees, so Joseph takes His body, wraps Him in linens, and places Him in a tomb. A large stone seals the tomb, and guards are posted to prevent anyone from stealing the body.

After the Jewish Sabbath day, Mary Magdalene and Mary, the mother of James, go to the tomb in the morning. An earthquake takes place, and an angel of the Lord rolls away the stone. Jesus is not in the tomb. The angel tells the women Jesus has risen from the dead. The guards at the tomb run to tell the chief priests what has happened. The elders decide to pay the guards to say the disciples had stolen the body in the middle of the night.

Jesus meets the women, and He instructs them to tell the remaining eleven disciples to meet Him in Galilee. When the eleven meet Jesus, He instructs them on baptism and obedience and reassures them that He would always be with them.

DISCUSSION

1. Jesus performs twenty-one miracles in the gospel of Matthew. He didn't perform miracles just because He could or to prove He was the Son of God. The healing, driving out demons, and controlling the weather is all done to show the world that He is sent to do for us what we cannot. God sent Jesus to all of us to die for our sins and save us because we could not do that for ourselves. Discuss what this means to you personally.

2. What do you think of the role of John the Baptist? At first, many thought he was the Messiah, but his role was to pave the way for the Messiah. As John's part diminished, Jesus's increased. And this was God's design. Why do you think a man was needed to announce Jesus?

3. "But when you give to the needy, do not let your left hand know what your right hand is doing, so that your giving may be in secret. Then your Father, who sees what is done in secret, will reward you" (Matthew 6:3–4). Why do you think giving in secret is important to God?

4. "If anyone will not welcome you or listen to your words, shake the dust off your feet when you leave that home or town" (Matthew 10:14). What can we take away from these words of Christ? Jesus was talking specifically about those who refused to hear the Word of God. In what ways does this verse apply to our lives today? Discuss uses of Jesus's words in divine defense against issues such as body-shaming, bullying in the workplace, listening to braggarts on social media, and more.

THE GOSPEL OF MARK

A MAN NAMED JOHN MARK, WHO WAS ACQUAINTED WITH the disciple Peter, wrote the gospel of Mark. He also accompanied the apostle Paul on the first of his three missionary trips. Mark writes the gospel with the Roman reader in mind, omitting references to Jewish law and customs that would be of no interest to that audience. The fast-paced gospel of Mark is the first written and the shortest of all four. Mark is a great first gospel for newcomers to the Bible.

Mark omits the birth of Jesus and cuts straight to John the Baptist preparing the way for the Messiah. He baptizes Jesus, and then Satan tempts Jesus for forty days and nights. He begins calling His disciples and His teaching. Jesus calls a tax collector, Levi, by simply saying, "Follow me."

Levi follows Him, and he is renamed as Matthew. Many of the miracles performed by Jesus in the book of Matthew are also found in the book of Mark. Mark even adds three: Jesus casts out an unclean spirit, He heals a deaf-mute, and He also heals a blind man. However, the book does not contain as many parables as the book of Matthew.

The crowds follow Jesus, the Pharisees harass Him, and John the Baptist is murdered. Peter confesses Jesus is the Christ, and Jesus predicts His own death.

The last eight days are similar to Matthew but take up most of the second half of the gospel. The main theme of Mark centers on Jesus as the suffering servant. He speaks, performs miracles, and dies with the sacrifice of a servant. And this is why so much of the book is devoted to His last days on earth, making the ultimate sacrifice for all.

DISCUSSION

1. In this gospel, a few instances occur where Jesus instructs someone not to tell anyone He is the Messiah. Discuss and speculate why you think Jesus does this.

2. "For even the Son of Man did not come to be served, but to serve, and to give his life as a ransom for many" (Mark 10:45). Service is the central idea of the gospel of Mark. In what ways do you serve others? How does serving others feel in contrast to serving only your own needs? Do you think service brings you in line with God's divine plan for all of us?

3. Read Mark 6:1–6. Faith does not happen because we witness miracles, but miracles often happen when we have faith. Discuss how you feel about this.

4. God sent Jesus to earth to die for all of our sins. God didn't have to do this. God wanted to do it so we could be together with Him in heaven forever. We didn't earn this. God did this for us out of grace. Grace is something given without having earned it. Discuss how you feel about receiving something from God without having earned it.

THE GOSPEL OF LUKE

LUKE, A NON-JEWISH PHYSICIAN, WROTE THE GOSPEL OF Luke and the book of Acts as a two-part letter to a man named Theophilus. No one knows who Theophilus was, but it is speculated that he might have been a Roman official and perhaps had a say in the punishment of the apostle Paul. This gospel was written about AD 60 when Christianity was becoming more popular throughout the entire Roman Empire. Luke's message emphasizes that Jesus is a Savior for all people, not just Jews.

The gospel follows the same basic outline as the book of Mark, but with some unique aspects from Luke's point of view. Luke wants to let the reader know that he has carefully researched the events of the book. "Therefore, since I myself have carefully investigated everything from the beginning, it seemed good also to me to write an orderly account for you, most excellent Theophilus, so that you may know the certainty of the things you have been taught" (Luke 1:3–4).

Luke includes the story of the angel Gabriel, who first appears to the priest Zechariah, who is married to Elizabeth, a descendent of Aaron. He tells the priest they will have a son "in the spirit and power of Elijah" (Luke 1:17). His wife, who had been barren, will become pregnant and give birth to John the Baptist. Gabriel also visits Mary, the young virgin, to tell her she will have a son and name Him Jesus. Mary and Elizabeth are related to each other somehow, making Jesus and John relatives, probably cousins.

Most of the traditional story of Christmas is found in the gospel of Luke. Augustus Caesar, the emperor of Rome at the time of Jesus's birth, orders a census taken, and everyone must travel to his or her homeland. Joseph, Mary's husband, is from the line of David in Bethlehem, so Joseph and a heavily pregnant Mary must travel there to register. Mary gives birth in a manger while they are in Bethlehem. And an angel, probably Gabriel, appears a third time to tell the good news to the shepherds in the fields. They all hurry to see Him and are amazed.

Luke is the only gospel to account Jesus as a child. His family travels with many family members to Jerusalem for the annual Passover celebration. And while making the journey home, His parents realize Jesus is missing. They check with relatives but cannot find Him. Mary and Joseph go back to Jerusalem and finally find Jesus in the temple court, talking to the priests. He is twelve years old at the time. He asks them, "Didn't you know I had to be in my Father's house?" (Luke 2:49). It is an odd thing to say, and they don't understand it.

The gospel of Matthew lists the lineage of Jesus back to Abraham. Luke lists His lineage all the way back to Adam, pointing out that Jesus is the Savior for all people, not just the Jews through Abraham.

After Jesus's baptism and temptation by Satan, He returns to Nazareth, where He reads from the prophet Isaiah. Jesus tells the people He is the Messiah that Isaiah spoke of. Such a statement enrages everyone in the synagogue that all plan to take Jesus to a cliff and throw Him to His death. Jesus slips through the crowd and leaves.

The book of Luke omits some of Jesus's miracles and adds some, including raising a widow's dead son and healing the ear of a high priest's servant. Many parables are found only in Luke. The parable of the Good Samaritan and the Prodigal Son are unique to this gospel.

Luke is the only gospel to account for Jesus's appearance to two of his followers on the day He arose from the dead. On that Sunday, the two are walking on a path back to their home in Emmaus. No doubt they are talking about the recent events when Jesus appears to them. The men do not recognize Jesus, and they tell Him all that has happened. Jesus has dinner with them. Jesus breaks bread and gives thanks, and suddenly, as the two realize it is Jesus, He disappears.

DISCUSSION

1. In Luke, an angel of the Lord tells the shepherds in the fields of the good news, a Savior is born. What do you think is the significance of this? The angel didn't tell Herod the Great, Augustus Caesar, or even the Pharisees. The angel told the commoner, the peasant shepherds tending the sheep.

2. Luke mentions food many times in the gospel, with special emphasis on the tie between food and community with others. Discuss the ways having a meal with others opens dialogue, creates communion, and increases understanding.

3. Luke includes songs of praise: Mary's song, Zechariah's song, song of the angels, and song of Simeon. Praise and worship are important in the gospel of Luke. Why do you think the act of worship is significant?

4. "But Jesus often withdrew to lonely places and prayed" (Luke 5:16). Jesus spent time with God alone, praying. In our hurried, hectic world, what can we learn from Jesus regarding prayer? Do you wish you had more quiet time alone to pray and spend time with God? What changes in your schedule would it take to make this happen?

THE GOSPEL OF JOHN

"FOR GOD SO LOVED THE WORLD THAT HE GAVE HIS ONE
and only Son, that whoever believes in him shall not perish but have
eternal life" (John 3:16). The gospel of John is the last written, probably
around AD 80. John refers to himself in the book as "the disciple
whom Jesus loved." The disciple John strays from the synoptic gospels
chronological, straightforward account of the life and death of Jesus.
John provides the reader with Jesus's own words of identity and
glorification. The descriptively spiritual, symbolic writing illustrates
Jesus as God's Son.

John offers seven signs, key miracles as evidence that He is
God's Son.

1. Jesus turns water into wine. This is the first of Jesus's miracles,
   which He performs at a wedding. The wine is gone, and His
   mother tells Him as much. Jesus knew, by performing this
   first miracle, He would set in motion the events that would
   eventually lead to His death.

2. Jesus heals an official's son. While in Galilee, a royal
   official tells Jesus that His son was sick in Capernaum.
   Jesus heals the boy from afar. When the official arrives
   home, he learns the boy got better at the exact moment

Jesus told him that his son would live. Jesus isn't limited by physical location.

3. Jesus heals at the Bethesda Pool. On the Sabbath, Jesus heals a man who had been disabled for thirty-eight years. Jesus isn't limited by time.

4. Jesus feeds five thousand. This miracle is found in all four gospels. While Jesus is speaking to the group, evening comes, and instead of dispersing the group, Jesus blesses five loaves of bread and two fish, and it feeds the entire group with leftovers. Jesus is nourishment for the soul.

5. Jesus walks on water. This miracle shows that Jesus has no physical limitations.

6. Jesus heals a man blind since birth. Assuming the man or his parents are sinful and therefore responsible for his blindness, the people who witness the miracle healing learn that God creates these difficulties to demonstrate Himself in our lives.

7. Jesus raises Lazarus from the dead. Jesus is called to Lazarus while he is sick, but Jesus delays. By the time He arrives, Lazarus has been dead for four days. Even so, Jesus calls for Lazarus to come out of his tomb, and he does, still covered with burial shrouds. Even death is no match for Jesus!

John also includes the seven "I am" statements by Christ:

1. "I am the bread of life" (John 6:35).
2. "I am the light of the world" (John 8:12).
3. "I am the gate" (John 10:7).
4. "I am the good shepherd" (John 10:11).
5. "I am the resurrection and the life" (John 11:25).
6. "I am the way and the truth and the life" (John 14:6).
7. "I am the true vine, and my Father is the gardener" (John 15:1).

John also witnesses many interesting details and accounts not mentioned in the other gospels:

- In John 13, Jesus washes the disciples' feet before the Passover meal to set the example for them. He is teaching them to serve others.
- When Jesus is dying on the cross, He turns His mother over to his beloved disciple John to care for her for the remainder of her life.
- After Jesus's death, John accounts that Joseph of Arimathea is assisted by Nicodemus the Pharisee, who believes in Jesus. The two men quickly prepare His body with myrrh and shrouds and bury Him in an unused nearby tomb.

John wrote this gospel about fifty years after Christ's resurrection. "This is the disciple who testifies to these things and who wrote them down. We know that his testimony is true" (John 21:24). John must have been very young as a disciple to Christ, and after having lived the remainder of his life taking care of Jesus's mother and witnessing the turbulent beginnings of the church, he composes a beautiful and deeply spiritual gospel for the world.

DISCUSSION

1. John chooses to emphasize the spiritual side of Jesus. The other three gospels focus on his human side. Discuss the ways the four gospels complement each other in portraying an accurate account of Jesus.

2. Jesus explains the Holy Spirit in this gospel, referring to the counselor and spirit of truth as a guide that will be sent to all believers who love and obey Him. Read John 14:15–21 and John 16:5–16. Jesus explains the Holy Spirit in these verses. Discuss what the Holy Spirit means to you.

3. The Trinity—God the Father, Jesus the Son, and the Holy Spirit— can be confusing. Try to think of it as one person who has three different roles, or aspects of themselves. Discuss the different roles of yourself and others to gain a clearer understanding of this concept.

4. "I am the way and the truth and the life. No one comes to the Father except through me" (John 14:6). Jesus calls Himself the way. He tells us He is the only way to heaven. No other religion is based on the single action of one man, the resurrection of Christ. Other religions have important prophets and belief systems, but not one or another is based on what happened to a man born the Son of God, persecuted and crucified, and raised from the dead. Discuss your thoughts and feeling about this.

THE ACTS OF THE APOSTLES

THE PHYSICIAN LUKE WROTE THE BOOK OF ACTS, OR ACTS of the Apostles, as a sequel to his gospel of Luke. Acts accounts what happens in next thirty years following Jesus's crucifixion. The book is divided into two sections: the focus on Peter and his ministry in Jerusalem and Paul's ministry to the Gentiles in the far reaches of the Roman world (Acts 13).

The book begins with Jesus telling the disciples to wait for the Holy Spirit, and then He is taken up to heaven. Then the disciples turn to the housekeeping subject of only having eleven disciples since Judas hanged himself. They pray and choose a man named Matthias to replace him.

Ten days after Jesus's final ascension, many people gather in Jerusalem for the spring celebration of Pentecost. The apostles are together when a violent wind from heaven fills their house, and the Holy Spirit fills them. The Holy Spirit gives them the ability to speak in different languages in the region. With so many people from out of town, the Lord has given them the power to communicate with everyone in his or her language. Peter addresses the crowd, and the number of Jesus's followers increases from 120 to about 3,000 in one day.

Peter and John enter the temple to pray when they see a local crippled man begging at the entrance. Peter heals the man, and word of this spreads, exciting the people to listen to Peter. Their numbers increase to around five thousand. The high priests and Sadducees take note of this event and put them in jail.

The men spend the night in jail and are presented before the Sanhedrin the following day. Fearing an uprising, the counsel of the Sanhedrin warns them to stop preaching and lets them go. Once released, they continue to minister, heal the sick, and drive out demons.

Again jealousy fills the members of the Sanhedrin because of the attention the apostles are receiving, so they put them all in jail. During the night, however, an angel of the Lord releases them. Enraged, the Sanhedrin wants to execute them, but a Pharisee named Gamaliel talks to the counsel, "Therefore, in the present case I advise you: leave these men alone! Let them go! For if their purpose or activity is of human origin, it will fail. But if it is from God, you will not be able to stop these men; you will only find yourselves fighting against God" (Acts 5:38–39)

When the twelve men encounter a dispute over the distribution of food to the widows in Jerusalem, they decide it is time to delegate their responsibilities. Seven men are chosen to oversee the physical needs of the poor, while the apostles continue to focus on ministry.

Stephen is one of the seven. As he is preaching at the Synagogue of Freedmen, an argument breaks out. Stephen is accused of blasphemy and brought before the Sanhedrin. The Holy Spirit continues to speak through Stephen as he preaches to the high priests. The Sanhedrin is offended, but lacking the authority to execute Stephen, the counsel releases him to the angry mob to be stoned to death. Stephen becomes the first Christian martyr.

A Pharisee named Saul watches the stoning of Stephen in approval. Saul actively persecutes Jesus's followers and imprisons them. Knowing many of the followers were moving to cities outside Jerusalem, Saul writes to the city of Damascus, asking for members of the way (the new Jesus followers) to be handed over for imprisonment in Jerusalem. Saul is on his way to Damascus when the Lord appears to him. The Lord asks Saul why he is persecuting Him, and then Saul loses his eyesight.

His traveling companions help the blind Saul to Damascus, where he fasts for three days. God calls upon Anaias, a man living in Damascus, to go to Saul and restore his sight by filling him with the Holy Spirit. "The Lord said to Anaias, 'Go! This man is my chosen instrument to carry my name before the Gentiles and their kings and before the people of Israel'" (Acts 9:15).

Once healed, Saul stays in Damascus and begins to minister in the name of the Lord. When he returns to Jerusalem, he tries to join the apostles, but they fear him. However, Barnabas believes Saul, befriends him, and convinces the apostles of his authenticity. Together, Barnabas and Saul teach in the city of Antioch, where Jesus's followers are first called Christians.

Back in Jerusalem, King Herod Agrippa I, the governor of Judea, arrests the apostle Peter. King Herod succeeded Marcellus, who succeeded the infamous Pontius Pilate. During the night, an angel of the Lord releases Peter from jail.

When King Herod cannot find Peter, he executes his prison guards. Some time later King Herod is staying in Caesarea, making a speech, when a commoner calls out, proclaiming the king is the voice of God. When the king does not praise God, an angel of the Lord immediately destroys him.

Attention turns back to Saul, now called Paul. Barnabas

accompanies Paul on what will be the first of three mission trips originating in Antioch. They sail first to the island of Cyprus and then on to cities along the northeast coast of the Mediterranean Rim. As they preach, some cities welcome them and become Christ followers, and others reject them, causing them to flee.

When they return to Antioch, they tell the apostles about their successes and the Gentiles who received the message of Christ. During the meeting, an important matter comes up. A debate arises as to whether or not the new followers must be circumcised and essentially become Jewish first before becoming a Jesus follower. Paul speaks up, making the final decision that it will not be necessary to be circumcised to follow Jesus. Paul wants to make it as easy as possible for new believers.

Paul and Barnabas are planning a second mission trip when they get into a dispute, causing the two to part ways. Barnabas continues a ministry with John Mark (who wrote the second gospel), and Paul chooses Silas to accompany him.

Paul and Silas leave from Antioch and travel further west and north this time, passing through and preaching in the cities of Derbe, Lystra, Iconium, and Troas. They cross the Aegean Sea, sailing to Macedonia and the cities of Neapolis and Philippi.

In Philippi, Paul drives a demon out of a slave girl who was making money predicting the future. Her owners become enraged because they have lost their income source. An angry mob throws Paul and Silas into jail. During the night, as the two are singing and praising God, an earthquake releases them. Not only are they released from jail, their jailer is converted and becomes a Christ follower that same night.

After they leave the city, they travel through Thessalonica and Berea and venture into Athens. In Athens, Paul finds many idols and praises the people for being very religious. Paul ministers to the people, "For I as walked around and looked very closely at your objects of worship, I even found an altar with this inscription: TO AN UNKNOWN GOD. Now what you worship as something unknown I am going to proclaim to you" (Acts 17:23).

The Athenians had an altar for a just-in-case god. That is, just in case they missed a god, that god would not be offended by not having an altar. Paul uses this altar to his advantage to preach and recruit more Jesus followers.

On Paul's third and final mission trip, he again travels through the cities of Derbe, Lystra, and Iconium in Galatia, and this time he stops in the city of Ephesus. God works miracles through Paul, healing the sick and driving out evil spirits. He explains to some followers that they need to be baptized with the Holy Spirit. Paul's teaching persuade many people in Ephesus, so much so that it calls the attention of an idol manufacturer, Demetrius, who causes a riot in Ephesus when he brings this to the attention of others who are losing their profits in idol making. Paul narrowly escapes and moves on.

In the city of Troas, Paul raises Eutychus from the dead. Paul continues to travel through the cities in Macedonia in which he traveled during his second trip, and then he returns via same path. This trip ends in Jerusalem.

Shortly after Paul arrives in Jerusalem, he is arrested and beaten. He goes before the Sanhedrin. He insults the high priests and is ultimately transferred to the city of Caesarea. Governor Felix of Judea hears Paul but leaves him in prison for two years. In AD 60, Governor Festus, who seems to have more interest in Paul's case, replaces Governor Felix. Paul decides he wants his case appealed to Rome and heard by Emperor Nero Caesar.

Before being transferred, Governor Festus speaks with King

Herod Agrippa II over Galilee and Perea. King Agrippa speaks with Paul and says, if he hadn't appealed to Nero, he would have released him. Finally Paul is transferred to Rome, where he lives alone under guard for years until his case is heard. During his imprisonment, Paul routinely accepts visitors and ministers to them.

DISCUSSION

1. The Holy Spirit encourages the apostles to preach and protects them from harm. Have you seen evidence of the Holy Spirit in your life through encouragement and protection when you are following God's path and others are not?

2. Do you agree with the Pharisee Gamaliel when he said, if a man's words are from God, no man can stop him?

3. Following Jesus and preaching on his behalf was dangerous in the first century. In many parts of the world today, Christianity is still dangerous. Think about how safe you are to be able to spread the word of Jesus in your community. It's safe to invite someone to church. It's safe to have Bible study in your home or in public. Consider how God can use you to reach those who need Jesus in their lives.

4. What do you think would have happened if Paul and his companions hadn't traveled, spreading the word of Jesus to the distant areas of the Roman Empire? Do you think Christianity would have stayed local in Jerusalem? Would it have died out completely? Do you think spreading the word of Jesus is as important today as it was in the first century? Perhaps it is just as important, but in a different way. Discuss the possibilities.

A BRIEF HISTORY LESSON
(NOT FOUND IN THE BIBLE)

IT'S NECESSARY TO PAUSE BRIEFLY TO INCLUDE SOME information provided by early church historians, Flavius Josephus and Eusebius of Caesarea. These men supplemented information that was omitted from the Bible perhaps because the material was common knowledge to the people at the time.

Emperor Nero Caesar ruled Rome from AD 54 to 68. Due to his insanity and hatred of Christians, Nero burned down most of Rome in AD 64 and blamed it on the Christians. Many Christians were persecuted after this event. They were arrested, tortured, and murdered. Although not stated in the Bible, tradition says Nero's order beheaded Paul in AD 67 or 68. Peter was also crucified about this time. The Jewish Revolt began in AD 66. The revolt ended in AD 70 with the Romans cornering the Jewish people in the temple in Jerusalem and then finally destroying it.

THE EPISTLES

THE FINAL BOOKS OF THE BIBLE ARE EPISTLES, OR SIMPLY letters written from about AD 48 to 95. In the years after Jesus's death and resurrection, the apostles reached out to spread the word of Christ. They traveled, preached, and wrote letters. The Bible contains nine letters from the apostle Paul to churches he visited or had hoped to visit. It also contains four letters from Paul to specific individuals. Finally the Bible contains nine more letters written by other authors.

These letters are not necessarily in the order they were written. Some are written early, during the same time periods of the Gospels and Acts, and others were transcribed very late after the Jewish Revolt. I will briefly touch on each one of the epistles of the Bible.

ROMANS

Apostle Paul writes this letter to a congregation he yearned to visit. Paul never formally preaches in Rome, but he does make it there when he was imprisoned and his case was appealed to the emperor in Rome. Paul writes this letter during his third mission trip while in the city of Corinth, circa AD 57.

The book of Romans is a comprehensive letter explaining Jesus and the need for a Savior to a congregation of people who are completely unaware of Christ. Paul begins with a greeting and introduces the subject of universal sin, the need for salvation, and finally God's gift of Jesus as the final atonement for all sin. Paul also emphasizes service and the proper behavior of a follower of Christ.

1 CORINTHIANS

While in the city of Ephesus on his third missionary trip, Paul receives a letter from the church in Corinth. This church was established during Paul's second missionary trip in AD 51, and now four years later, there seems to be chaos in the congregation. They are asking for help and advice. Paul responds with the letter, 1 Corinthians.

Paul addresses the congregation in Corinth on several urgent matters. The church is divided on whom to follow—Jesus, Paul, the apostle Peter, or Apollos (a local outspoken preacher.) Paul makes it clear to only follow Jesus. Other problems include a man who is sleeping with his father's wife and an amassment of lawsuits among congregation members, and the Holy Communion has become a feast favoring the wealthy. Paul advises on all matters and also clears up an apparent dispute about the details concerning the resurrection.

2 CORINTHIANS

Paul writes 2 Corinthians about a year after writing the first letter. Scholars believe as many as five letters were written to the church in Corinth, but only two made it into the Bible. Between the first and second letters, Paul visits Corinth and is horribly rejected by them. Paul is called a false apostle and leaves. This letter represents an appeal to restore harmony between himself and the church in Corinth.

Paul reveals in this letter, "To keep me from becoming conceited because of these surpassingly great revelations, there was given me a thorn in my flesh, a messenger of Satan, to torment me" (2 Corinthians 12:7). There is speculation as to what Paul's thorn is, but many believe it to be his poor eyesight.

GALATIANS

This letter to the churches of Galatia is probably Paul's first letter, written in AD 49. The Galatians are being influenced by Jewish-Christians who insist it is necessary to become circumcised under the law of Moses before becoming Christians. Paul instructs them that faith in the Holy Spirit is more important than observing this Jewish law.

EPHESIANS

Ephesians is one of the four prison epistles Paul wrote while imprisoned in Rome. The other three are Philippians, Colossians, and Philemon. Ephesians 1–3 focuses on the doctrine principles of Christ, and the last three chapters focus on morality and good behavior in the home among family. "Be imitators of God, therefore, as dearly loved children" (Ephesians 5:1).

PHILIPPIANS

Philippi is the city where Paul was in jail and set free by an earthquake. The jailer himself is converted to Christianity. Now Paul is in prison again, this time in Rome, and he writes an uplifting letter to the church founded in Philippi. Paul writes, "Now I want to you to know, brothers, that what has happened to me has really served to advance the gospel. As a result, it has become clear throughout the whole palace guard and to everyone else that I am in chains for Christ" (Philippians 1:12–13).

COLOSSIANS

Christianity was founded in the city of Colosse during Paul's third missionary trip. Paul is actually in the city of Ephesus when he sends a traveling companion, Epaphras, to the nearby city of Colosse. Epaphras sets up the church in Colosse.

While in prison in Rome, Paul begins to hear rumors of false preaching in Colosse, and he becomes concerned about them. This letter reminds the Colossians that Jesus is superior to all. Paul also stresses good behavior within the family unit.

1 THESSALONIANS

This letter is probably Paul's second letter after Galatians. After Paul establishes the church here, he is forced to leave quickly. Paul moves on to other cities, but he still worries about the congregation in Thessalonica. A young, probably teenaged, companion of Paul's reports to him that the church is doing well. A pleased Paul writes this letter of support to them.

2 THESSALONIANS

Written soon after 1 Thessalonians, Paul receives word that a rumor is being spread in Thessalonica regarding the end of times. Apparently they believe the end has already begun. Some are upset, and others have even stopped working. Paul writes to reassure them that the end has not begun and to tell them to continue work as usual.

1 TIMOTHY

1 Timothy is the first of three pastoral epistles. 2 Timothy and Titus are the others. All three are directed to a church leader with specific instructions on how to care for their congregation.

Paul has appointed Timothy to stay in the city of Ephesus and take care of the young church. In about AD 63, Paul writes to Timothy and instructs him on the subjects of false teachers and ways to interact with different congregation members. Paul also gives Timothy encouragement.

2 TIMOTHY

In AD 67, Paul writes this last letter before his own death. Paul says good-bye to Timothy, knowing he will soon be executed.

TITUS

Paul puts Titus in charge of the church on the island of Crete. The people of Crete have a bad reputation so Paul knows Titus may need his advice. Paul explains to Titus in the letter what to teach and how to instruct the different groups of people on the island.

PHILEMON

Paul is writing to the leader, Philemon, who runs a church from his home. Philemon owns a slave, Onesimus, who ran away, met up with Paul, and became a Christian. Paul appeals to Philemon to welcome Onesimus home as a brother rather than a runaway slave.

HEBREWS

The author of Hebrews is unknown. It was probably written a year or two before the temple destruction in AD 70. After the AD 64 fire set by Emperor Nero, Christian persecutions increased dramatically, making Christianity more dangerous than ever.

As the name of this book suggests, the letter is addressed to Jewish Christians struggling with their new faith. People are falling back into their old ways of Jewish rituals and sacrifices, but the author reminds them that the sacrifice of Christ supersedes these old practices. Jesus came as a final sacrifice, making this new covenant superior to the old covenant with Abraham and the Hebrew people.

JAMES

Jesus's mother and her husband Joseph had four more sons after Jesus. They also had at least two daughters. One son was James, the brother of Jesus. James wrote this letter from Jerusalem to all the Jewish Christians in the surrounding regions. The date of the letter is uncertain, anywhere from AD 45 to 65.

James calls upon the new followers to be more than faithful. He urges them to demonstrate their faith through good works. Doing good works for others finishes the work God has begun in them. "Consider it pure joy, my brothers, whenever you face trials of many kinds, because you know that the testing of your faith develops perseverance. Perseverance must finish its work so that you may be mature and complete, not lacking anything" (James 1:2–4).

1 PETER

Not only is Peter one of Jesus's apostles, he is also the first leader of the Roman Catholic church. Jesus tells Peter in the gospel of Matthew, "And I tell you that you are Peter, and on this rock I will build my church, and the gates of Hades will not overcome it" (Matthew 16:18).

Writing this letter from the city of Rome (for which Peter uses the code name "Babylon"), he addresses the Gentiles in the far corners of the Roman world. Peter preaches of the persecution of Christians, telling them to be prepared for the suffering they will endure.

2 PETER

Peter writes this letter in the late AD 60s. He knows his execution is near. Peter is writing this epistle because he is concerned about false teaching within the church. He reassures them that there will be retribution for this heresy. Peter also gives a peek into the second coming of the Lord and the end of days.

1 JOHN

The apostle John, the one whom Jesus loved, wrote these next three letters. John died circa AD 100 and may have been the only apostle to die of natural causes. He witnessed the birth and growth of Christianity to the far reaches of the Roman Empire. He also observed years of persecution.

The three letters were written in AD 92, approximately sixty years after the crucifixion of Jesus. Most of the eyewitnesses have died by this time, leaving some new preachers with a secondhand—or thirdhand—version of the original events surrounding Christ. It's much like a game of telephone where a player whispers a message to the next, but the end message emerges far from the original message. Perhaps that is happening in the church at this time.

John addresses false teachers who are preaching that Jesus appeared only in spirit form, perhaps without a physical body. Others are saying that Jesus was not actually God's son. John corrects these false beliefs in this letter.

2 JOHN

John addresses the church as a lady in this epistle. In this short letter, John warns of deceivers in the church "who do not acknowledge Jesus Christ as coming in the flesh" (2 John 7).

3 JOHN

In another short letter, John addresses his friend Gaius and reminds him to show generosity and accommodation to those passing through the area.

JUDE

Jude was the brother of Jesus, born to Mary and Joseph. In this short epistle, Jude also warns against false teachings within the church.

Interestingly Jude introduces the second of only two of God's named archangels in the Bible. The word "archangel" simply means a high-ranking angel of the Lord. In this letter, Jude reports the Archangel Michael to have fought Satan for the body of Moses after his death. The Archangel Gabriel in the gospel of John is the other named angel in the Bible.

APOCALYPTIC BOOK
REVELATION

The book of Revelation stands apart because it is the only example of apocalyptic writing. The word "apocalypse" from the Greek work *apokalypsis* simply means "secret information revealed" about future events. John had lived in Ephesus, but sometime during the reign of Roman Emperor Domitian, John was persecuted for his ministry and exiled to the small Mediterranean island of Patmos. Here in Patmos, John receives the revelation vision and writes what will become the final book of the Bible.

The year is AD 95 when John writes to seven churches on the mainland of Asia. He addresses the congregations in Ephesus, Smyrna, Pergamum, Thyatira, Sardis, Philadelphia, and Laodicea. The number seven is symbolic and repeated many times in this book.

In John's vision, Jesus appears to him and instructs him to write down everything he sees. John is standing in front of an open door to heaven. He enters and sees what appears to be a slain lamb, who is Jesus. Jesus is the only one worthy to open a scroll of seven seals. One by one, each seal is opened. The first four are the four horsemen of the apocalypse. The horses are white, red, black, and pale. Each seal unleashes plagues, earthquakes, firestorms, and famine upon humanity. Before the seventh seal is opened, an angel asks to mark those on earth who are called to serve. The number called to serve is 144,000, or 12,000 from each of the tribes of Israel.

The seventh seal is opened. Silence falls. Then a judgment is unleashed against humanity. Hail, fire, and other atrocities kill one-third of all people on earth. "The rest of mankind that were not killed by these plagues still did not repent of the work of their hands" (Revelation 9:20).

Seeing a pause in this happening, John writes about a woman who gives birth to a son, presumably Jesus. Standing before her, ready to pounce as she gives birth is a dragon, or Satan. The child and woman are rescued, but the dragon wages a war on all of her other children, Jesus's followers. Then John witnesses two beasts, one from the sea and another from the earth. The number of the beast is revealed in this book as 666.

John sees a white horse whose rider is Jesus coming to earth a second time. A battle against Satan is won, and the ancient serpent is thrown into the abyss, which is sealed for a thousand years. After the thousand years, Satan is released, but his deceit of man is judged, and he is tormented forever.

A perfect new heaven and earth are created. "The grace of the Lord Jesus be with God's people. Amen" (Revelation 22:21).

DISCUSSION

1. What do you think about Paul's transformation from a Pharisee and persecutor of Christians to an apostle of Christ? What does this mean for any one of us? What does this mean to you?

2. Philemon meets with other Christians in his home. This is one of earliest accounts of Christians meeting together in a home to worship. Do you go to church every Sunday? Do you belong to a group of Christians who meet outside of the official church building on Sundays? Consider the benefits of this additional interaction with those who follow Christ, and discuss removing any obstacles to nurturing a relationship with Christ.

3. Consider that the apostle John began life as a young fisherman, followed Jesus, took care of Jesus's mother, wrote a gospel, and then wrote the book of Revelation before his death around the age of one hundred. John's character developed as he aged, immersing himself in following Christ with all of his heart. Discuss this ripening of spirit in John and what this means for your own potential in life.

4. "Here I am! I stand at the door and knock. If anyone hears my voice and opens the door, I will come in and eat with him, and he with me" (Revelation 3:20). Christ instructs John to write these words to the church in Laodicea. What do these words mean to you? How do they make you feel?

CONCLUSION

"'I AM THE ALPHA AND THE OMEGA,' SAYS THE LORD GOD, 'who is, and who was, and who is to come, the Almighty'" (Revelation 1:8). God tells us He is the beginning and the end. He is everything. God created us with free will, and we sinned. The original sin of Adam and Eve separated us from God. But that wasn't the end of the story. It was the beginning.

We ran away from God, but God wanted us back. Over and over again, we sinned, and He worked on our behalf to bring us back to Him. Finally God sent His only Son as a final sacrifice on our behalf. Notice that the Savior sought us out and came to earth to live among us. The entire Bible is the glorious story of our heavenly Father working on our behalf to bring every last one of us home to Him.

Then Jesus told them this parable: "Suppose one of you has a hundred sheep and loses one of them. Does he not leave the ninety-nine in the open country and go after the lost sheep until he finds it? And when he finds it, he joyfully puts it on his shoulders and goes home. Then he calls his friends and neighbors together and says, 'Rejoice with me; I have found my last sheep.' I tell you that in the same way there will be more rejoicing in heaven over one sinner who repents than over ninety-nine righteous persons who do not need to repent" (Luke 15:3–7).

OLD TESTAMENT

MEDITERRANEAN SEA

SEA OF GALILEE

ISRAEL/
CANAAN

JORDAN RIVER

AMMON

DEAD SEA

MOAB

PHILISTINE

EDOM

EGYPT

NILE RIVER

RED
SEA

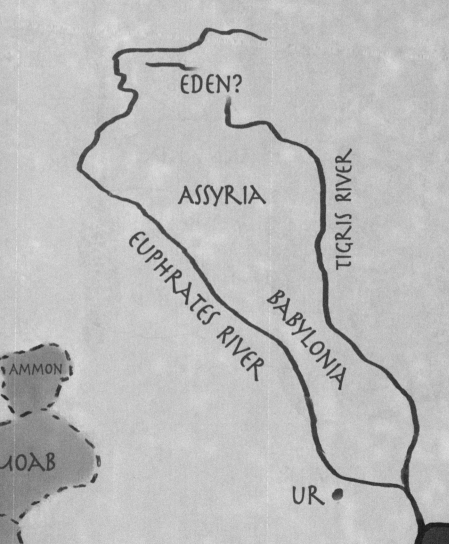

EDEN?

ASSYRIA

TIGRIS RIVER

EUPHRATES RIVER

BABYLONIA

AMMON

MOAB

DOM

UR •

PERSIAN GULF

THE GOSPELS

GALILEE

SEA OF GALILEE

CAPERNAUM
NAZARETH

JORDAN RIVER

MEDITERRANEAN
SEA

SAMARIA

JERUSALEM

JUDEA

DEAD SEA

BETHLEHEM

EGYPT

NILE RIVER

RED

SEA

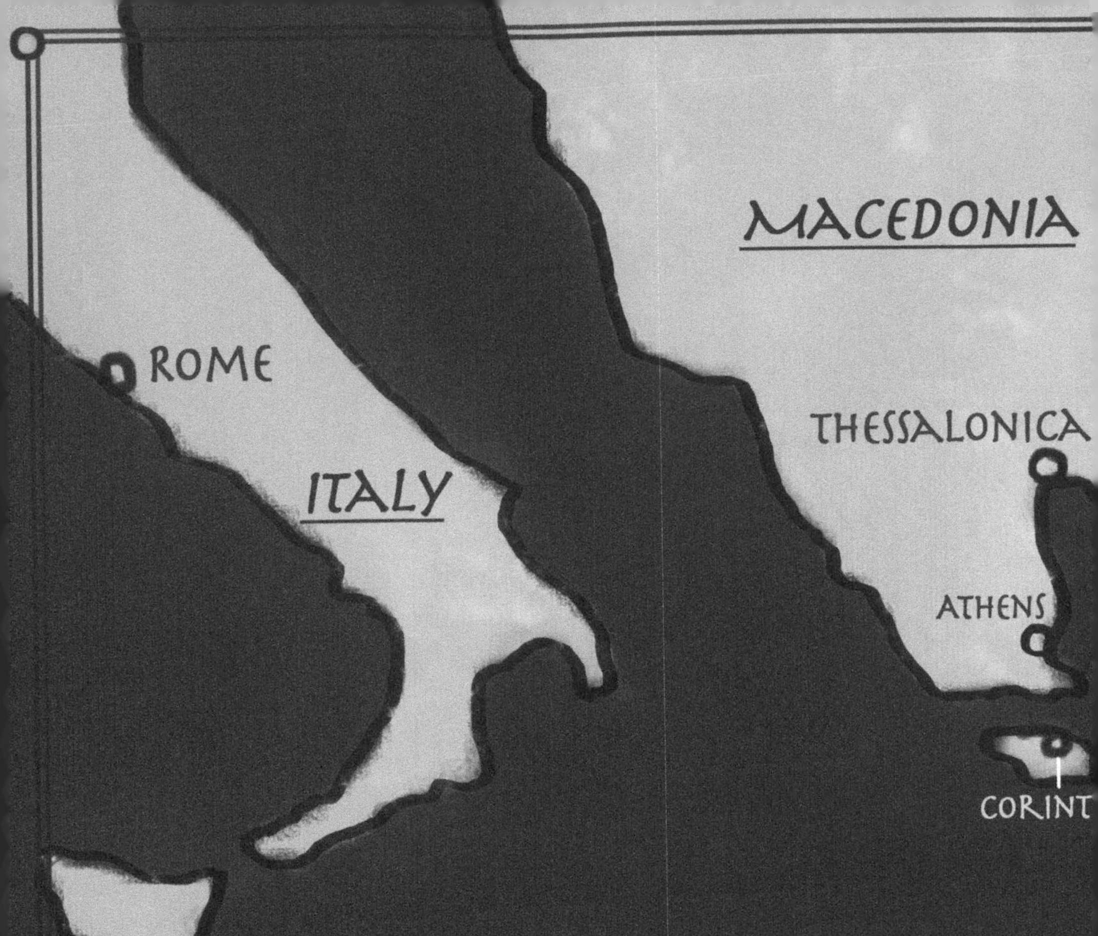

ACTS & MISSIONS

ACTS & MISSIONS

...CONTINUED

GALATIA

PHILIPPI

TROAS

COLOSSE   LYSTRA

EPHESUS   TARSUS

PATMOS   ANTIOCH

CRETE   CYPRUS

                              DAMASCUS

MEDITERRANEAN SEA

                    JERUSALEM

NILE
RIVER

EGYPT

                              RED SEA

Printed in the United States
By Bookmasters